Ulrich Klinge

TRAINING
Success in English
Grammar, Vocabulary, Spelling
Sekundarstufe II

Beilage: Lösungsheft

Ernst Klett Verlag
Stuttgart Düsseldorf Leipzig

Quellennachweis

S. 12:
The Art of Cartooning. 75 Years of American Magazine. The Cartoonist's Guild. Ch. Scribner's Sons, New York 1975

S. 15, 100:
Peanuts Classics by Ch. Schulz. United Feature Syndicate. Holt Rinehart and Winston, New York. o. S. © k/s Presse-Illustrations-Bureau, Kopenhagen.

S. 25, 65 o., 65 u., 86:
Hard Sell. Punch Among the Commercials. © Grafton Books, London 1989, o. S.

S. 20, 29, 32, 33, 35, 36, 38, 63:
Animals, Animals, Animals. Harper & Row, Publishers, New York 1979.

S. 41, 49:
Animals, Animals, Animals. Harper & Row, Publishers, New York 1979, S. 157, 55. © The New Yorker Magazine Inc., New York.

S. 45:
Class War. Punch in the Schoolroom. © Grafton Books, London 1988, o. S.

S. 56, 83:
Sporting Gestures. Punch Plays the Game. © Grafton Books, London 1988, o. S.

Die Deutsche Bibliothek – CIP-Einheitsaufnahme

Klinge Ulrich:
Training Success in English: Grammar, Vocabulary, Spelling ;
Sekundarstufe II / Ulrich Klinge. – 6. Aufl. – Stuttgart ;
Düsseldorf ; Leipzig : Klett, 1998
ISBN 3-12-922112-3

6. Auflage 1998

Internetadresse: http://www.klett.de
Satz: G. Müller, Heilbronn
Druck: Wilhelm Röck, Weinsberg
Innengestaltung: Hitz und Mahn, Stuttgart
Einbandgestaltung: Bayerl & Ost, Frankfurt/M.
ISBN 3-12-922112-3

Inhalt

Einleitung

Kennen Sie die Situation?

Unseren Englischunterricht mag ich eigentlich ganz gern, die Themen sind oft interessant, zu vielen Fragen könnte ich was sagen ... wenn ich es auf Deutsch tun dürfte ... auf Englisch mache ich einfach zu viele Fehler ... und was ich sage, hört sich immer so einfach und banal an.

Und überhaupt: die ewigen Fehler verderben mir dauernd die Note in der Klausur! Ich würde schon „was für Englisch tun", wenn ich nur wüßte, wo ich anfangen sollte ...

Was Sie in diesem Buch finden

Dieses Buch ist entstanden aus einer langjährigen Auswertung typischer Fehler, die deutschsprachige Schülerinnen und Schüler in ihren Englischklausuren gemacht haben.

Es ist gedacht für die Sekundarstufe II; es will denen helfen, die ihre Sicherheit in englischer Rechtschreibung und Grammatik verbessern und ihr Ausdrucksvermögen in mündlichen und schriftlichen Äußerungen trainieren und erweitern wollen.

Anders als viele Übungsbücher zielt es nicht auf Vollständigkeit, sondern konzentriert sich auf Bereiche, die für deutschsprachige Englischlerner besonders fehleranfällig sind, wie z. B. Adjektive/Adverbien, Konditionalsätze, Wortstellung, usw. Im Wortschatz- und Ausdrucksbereich bietet es Lösungen an für Redewendungen und Aussageintentionen, die Schülerinnen und Schüler in ihren Englischklausuren häufig benötigen und vom Deutschen her oft falsch „übersetzen".

Das Buch ist aufgebaut nach dem Prinzip steigender Schwierigkeiten: die Übungen „ohne Stern" sind als überwiegend einfach, die mit einem Stern (*) gekennzeichneten als mittelschwer, die mit zwei Sternen (**) als eher anspruchsvoll einzustufen. Die verschiedenen Niveaus entsprechen in etwa den Klassenstufen 10/11 bzw. 12 und 13.

Wie arbeiten Sie mit dem Buch?

Zu Beginn der Übungen können Sie in einem Einstiegstest (auf S. 7) Ihr Wissen überprüfen. Wahrscheinlich kennen Sie aber Ihre Schwächen in bestimmten Teilgebieten bereits, oder Ihr(e) Kurslehrer(in) hat Sie auf „Ihre" Fehlerbereiche hingewiesen. In diesem Fall können Sie die entsprechenden Übungskapitel gezielt aufsuchen. Legen Sie eine gute Englischgrammatik für die *grammar chapters* und ein verläßliches Wörterbuch für die *spelling* und *vocabulary chapters* bereit, um in Zweifelsfragen jederzeit nachschlagen zu können. Beginnen Sie auf dem Ihnen angemessenen Lernniveau (Sternchen!), und arbeiten Sie die einzelnen Übungen grundsätzlich schriftlich durch. Dabei gilt das Prinzip: lieber weniger Übungen vollständig als viele Übungen ein bißchen und mit vielen Lücken! Vergleichen Sie erst dann Ihre Antworten mit denen im Lösungsheft.

Wiederholen Sie die wichtigsten Übungen nach einiger Zeit, am besten mehrmals. Vor allem wenn die nächste Kursarbeit ansteht, sollten Sie Ihre Kenntnisse nochmals auffrischen. Auf diese Weise werden Sie Ihre sprachliche Sicherheit spürbar erhöhen und Ihr Ausdrucksvermögen deutlich verbessern.

Selbstverständlich können Sie das Trainingsbuch auch systematisch durchgehen. Sie nehmen sich einen bestimmten Zeitraum vor und beschäftigen sich regelmäßig ein- bis zweimal pro Woche mit den angebotenen Themen und Übungen.

Die Revisionstests am Ende des Bandes sollen Sie motivieren, Ihre Fortschritte selbst zu überprüfen. Die „zehn Todsünden“ des Grundkursschülers machen Sie noch einmal auf die erfahrungsgemäß häufigsten Fehlerquellen für deutschsprachige Englischlerner aufmerksam.

Und nun viel Erfolg beim Lösen der Aufgaben!

Überprüfen Sie Ihr Wissen

Part 1

a or **an**

Spot the mistakes.

1. an excellent author
2. an European country
3. an university
4. it's a great honour for me
5. a honourable man

Part 2

You meet false friends: be careful!

1. *(Meinung)*
   Give me your .... on British football.
2. *(Bedeutung)*
   What is the .... of the word 'symbol'?
3. *(erinnert mich an)*
   That song .... of the Beatles.
4. *(euch erinnern)*
   Can you .... what we did last week?
5. *(interessiert)*
   The class was not .... in what the teacher said.

Part 3

Translate. Keep special attention to <u>conditional clauses</u>.

1. Was würdest du tun, wenn jemand dir $ 1.000 geben würde?
2. Wenn ich noch mal jung wäre, würde ich viele Dinge anders machen.
3. Er wäre gekommen, wenn wir ihn eingeladen hätten.
4. Wenn du uns alles erzählt hättest, wären wir nicht so überrascht worden.
5. Ich würde es nicht behaupten *(to claim s.th.)*, wenn ich es nicht wüßte.

Part 4

Make sure of your vocabulary.

1. *(typisch für)*
   The 'can – do' spirit is .... the way many Americans see themselves.
2. *(hängt ab von)*
   Your success in life .... a lot of factors.
3. *(betrachtet werden als)*
   She can be .... a feminist author.
4. *(u. a.)*
   You'll have to do, ..., a translation this time.
5. *(bringt)*
   This author .... quite a few facts in his article.
6. *(daraus folgt)*
   Our best player is injured; .... we'll probably lose our match.
7. *(bezieht sich auf)*
   The author .... the political situation in our country.
8. *(kann eingeteilt werden in)*
   The text .... four units.
9. *(umfaßt)*
   The last unit .... ll. 35–44.
10. *(zeigt sich)*
    The author's view .... from the very beginning.

Part 5

Do you know your prepositions?

1. Have you already read "The Secret Diary of A. Mole Aged 13¾" ..... Sue Townsend?
2. It deals ..... the experiences written down ..... a British youngster ..... the lower classes.
3. He lives ..... his parents and is interested ..... social work.
4. He looks ..... an old man who is very lonely and who lives all ..... himself.
5. We could discuss ..... a lot of passages ..... that book.
6. Read that interesting book and you will agree ..... me.

Part 6

Spot the one spelling mistake in each sentence.

1. You should allways pay attention when s.th. important is said.
2. She is, I believe, taller then her brother.
3. Can you discribe what the place actually looks like?
4. Most familys have not more than two children.
5. I cannot except your offer. Sorry!
6. There is an other point I'd like to mention.
7. Parents have a lot of responsability for their kids.
8. How did live on earth begin?
9. That doesn't make sence to me.
10. He is quite a charakter.

Part 7

adjective or **adverb**

Translate the following sentences.

1. Sie sah ihn freundlich an.
2. Das wird mir jetzt klar *(to me!)*
3. Das ist ganz klar ein Problem, über das wir reden müssen.
4. Er beschreibt den Mann detailliert.
5. Der Autor spricht den Leser direkt an.

Part 8

Give a synonym (= word or expression of similar meaning).

1. Finally the visitors arrived.
2. Do you share the standpoint that punks are dangerous?
3. Have you reached your aim/goal?
4. Can you give proof of that?

5. This is what the author wants to make clear to us.
6. The text can be divided into three major units.
7. The main part reaches from ... to ...
8. The text is to illustrate the dangers of drug abuse.
9. In my opinion that's rubbish *(„Blödsinn")*!
10. To begin with we'll read out the text.

Part 9

Translate these stock phrases.

a)

1. If I'm not mistaken ...
2. As far as I'm concerned ...
3. To be quite frank ...
4. By the way ...
5. There is no denying that ...

b)

1. Wie soll ich mich ausdrücken ...?
2. Ich muß zugeben, daß ...
3. Abgesehen von ...
4. Um zur Sache zu kommen ...
5. Einerseits ..... andererseits ...

Part 10

Translate these sentences. Make sure your construction of the passive voice is correct.

1. Englisch wird von Piloten in der ganzen Welt gesprochen.
2. Die Maschine ist nicht überprüft worden *(to check)*.
3. Die Sicherheitsgurte müssen angelegt werden.
4. Drinks werden erst während des Fluges serviert.
5. Dieser Flughafen wurde vor 10 Jahren gebaut.

Points total: 72

Points scored:

Spelling

Exercise 1

Spot the spelling mistakes in each sentence.

1. She realy wanted to understand his motive for saying no.
2. We should allways drive carefully.
3. My parents try to fullfill most of my wishes.
4. This hamburger tastes awfull.
5. Peter and Mary have decided to seperate.
6. I'm going to discribe the author's intention first.
7. Today we'll begin by studying Master Turner's charakter.
8. In reality she looks much better then on the photo.
9. I can't except the author's oppinion on education.
10. You cannot leave children to themselfs.
11. An other point I do not understand is why parents do so little to control there kids.
12. I cannot belive that parents do not realize that.

Exercise 2

a) **s** **or** **c**

1. That doesn't make sen … e.
2. In his presen … e we had to be quiet.
3. That sounds absolutely sen … ele … .
4. Her absen … e was not noticed.
5. Have you understood the last senten … e?
6. He speaks with a foreign a … ent.
7. He is a sen … ible young man.
8. I'd like to be one hundred per … ent sure.

Complete the inscription on the poster by adding the missing letters.

b) **o** or **oo**

1. That can easily be pro...ed from the text.
2. The pro... of the pudding is in the eating.
3. Can you pro...e me wrong?
4. We don't want to lo...se the match.
5. Gains and lo...s
6. Have you lo... your memory?
7. Nobody likes being considered as a lo...er.
8. He grieved for the lo... of his friend.

c) **i – ie – y**

1. We've got two 'Jims' in our famil... .
2. More and more children come from broken famil...s.
3. Our famil...'s favourite pastime is watching TV.
4. He is a famil...-man.
5. Most famil...s' main concern is money.
6. Pat is the new part...-spokesman.

7. The part...'s new leader is quite unknown.
8. We've got four major part...s in our country.
9. The part...s' foremost problem is raising money.

d) **e – i – ie – ee – ea – y**

1. In his famous poem Carl Sandburg d...scr...bes the city of Chicago.
2. This model is on d...splay only.
3. The text d...v...des into several stanzas.
4. He d...d of cancer.
5. The mother caught her child l...ing.
6. The baby cr...d bitterly.
7. There's no use cr...ing over spilt milk.
8. He is a human b...ing after all.
9. He was too w...k to walk alone.
10. 'Newsw...k' is a w...kly n...ws magazine published in the U.S.
11. Can you expl...n the word 'expl...n...tion'?
12. I b...l...v... that 'in my b...l...' is written with one '...' only.

e) **de** or **di**

1. d...vide
2. d...saster
3. d...sinterested
4. d...scribe
5. d...spair
6. d...sillusion
7. d...stroy
8. d...sarmament
9. d...spite
10. d...segregation
11. d...sintegration
12. d...suse
13. d...viation
14. d...ssimilar
15. d...visive factor

Exercise 3

Examine the verbs and spot the spelling mistakes.

1. He answerd in a whisper.
2. She speakes of going to Britain for a year.
3. The traffic lights were red. We stoped at once.
4. My friend has developed a taste for hard rock music.
5. Our teacher talkes with a foreign accent.
6. We've build up a good relationship to our teacher.
7. Where have you learnt to speak Japanese?
8. He watchs TV till late at night.
9. They havn't made it in time.
10. The author describes the hotel in detail.
11. I can not but agree with you.
12. He reachs the main road.

Exercise 4

a) life or live

1. Our friend li...s next door.
2. Li...ing conditions are bad.
3. The American way of li... .
4. The match was televised li... .
5. They gave her the kiss of li... .
6. That's li... .
7. They had the time of their li... .
8. We should all li...e in harmony.
9. A decent standard of li...ing.
10. How did li... begin?

b) self or selves

1. They must try it themsel... .
2. He will do it hi...sel... .
3. Let's do it oursel... .
4. The baby it...sel... could hold its feeding bottle.
5. Too much sel...ishness is a bad feature, isn't it?

Revision

Read this text and mark 16 spelling mistakes.

Lets consider television and it's development in the next few years. People will discribe it as a 'reinvention of television'. A viewer of the 21st century will not belive that there once where TV sets that merely showed programmes without viewer interaction. As a first step television will establish a new norm (HDTV). This norm will provide more colourfull spectacles and match the quality of motion pictures. An other development will be the optical disc, a brother of the compact disc, that can display photographs, moving video, computer data and printed text. You havn't heard of interactive travelogue discs yet? It is an electronic guide who's range of information is enormous. As the tourist roams through London, for example, he watchs selected programmes and at the same time he can request any information he is intrested in. So, at last, he is realy free to discover London, or other places, on his own. Oppinions on that will, of course, be devided. You can not deny, however, that these are exciting prospects about television in the future. The question is how we will adapt to these rapid changes and there consequences.

Grammar

Article and Determiners

Exercise 1

a or **an**

1. ..... author
2. ..... British author
3. ..... great authority
4. ..... hotel
5. ..... American hotel
6. ..... European hotel
7. ..... hour or two
8. ..... quarter of ..... hour
9. it's ..... honour for me
10. it's ..... great honour for me
11. ..... university
12. ..... united Europe
13. ..... unusual university
14. ..... usually practised method
15. ..... unborn baby

Exercise 2

a) **this** or **these**

1. I need .... information for the report I have to write.
2. Come and look at .... exotic birds: they are very pretty.
3. Would you prefer .... book here or the one we've got over there?
4. I'm afraid of .... people; they look a bit dangerous.
5. You do not understand .... question? Let me explain it then.
6. Listen to .... news item: over 500 people killed in the plane crash.
7. Are .... men from Britain?
8. In all .... years I have never forgotten her.

b) this or these

Spot the mistake. (Some sentences are correct.)

1. This is what I've always wanted to know.
2. This people are wearing funny clothes indeed.
3. These information may be important to you.
4. You want me to put this question again? Listen then.
5. Do you meet this men every day?
6. One of this days I'll make a trip to Florida.
7. I like this type of people very much.
8. This are the men the police have been looking for.

*Exercise 3

a) the or 'zero'-article

1. He had all ..... time he needed.
2. ..... time is money.
3. What is ..... time, please?
4. At ..... time of Shakespeare.
5. Let's study the theme of ..... time in our story.
6. That is an image taken from ..... nature.
7. In their boat the men struggled against the fores of ..... nature.
8. It is in ..... nature of things that man is curious.

b)

1. ..... death of his father
2. Do you fear ..... death?
3. ..... death is waiting for you around the corner.
4. Have you heard about ..... sudden death of Tom's uncle?
5. ..... death I fear most is dying from cancer.

c)

1. ..... society we live in
2. ..... society of the 1990ies
3. He is against the way ..... society is run.
4. ..... British society is tripartite.
5. Who are the opinion leaders of ..... society?
6. He is often seen in ..... society.

d)

1. ..... man is mortal.
2. ..... only man I can rely on is my father.
3. ..... man in the street
4. That is ..... man I've been looking for.
5. ..... man has proved unreasonable more than once in the long history of ..... mankind.
6. Our world is based on ..... science.
7. ..... science of our age develops fast.
8. Are you interested in ..... science of the Middle Ages?
9. It is ..... scientist's job to deal with ..... science.

Adjective vs. Adverb

Exercise 1

Complete these sentences. (Some are correct.)

a)

1. The meaning of the text will become clear..... if you listen once more.
2. Let me say this very clear..... .
3. That is absolute..... clear..... .
4. You are clear..... wrong about that.

5. He tried to make it clear..... to us where he stood.
6. That is clear..... a problem we have to consider.
7. Have you got a clear..... conscience?
8. Speak more clear..... if you want us to understand you.

b)

1. Normal..... Dr Watson serves as Sherlock Holmes' assistant.
2. In 'The Hound of the Baskervilles', however, he does not play his normal..... role.
3. The role Watson plays here seems normal..... but, actually, it is far from normal: he himself conducts the investigation.
4. Final..... Holmes explains the solution of the puzzle ..... detailed ..... ; i.e. Holmes' report is very detailed.
5. Holmes finds his solution quite eas......
6. That would not be eas..... for normal..... people.

***Exercise 2**

Check the <u>adjectives</u> and/or <u>adverbs</u> and spot the mistake. (Some sentences are correct.)

1. The difficulties with my parents are much more greater now than they were in the past.
2. My father is an extreme difficult person to get along with.
3. What you are saying about your father is clearly wrong.
4. That is the absolutely climax of the story.
5. We should try everything we can think of to resolve the problem peaceful.
6. That part of Northern Ireland looks quite peaceful.
7. I should like to have much more friends than I have now.
8. Normally I mean what I say: you should take me serious.
9. Children all over the world are differently and, therefore, need different kinds of help.
10. The most parents are too intolerant.

"Everybody hang on ..... *(richtig fest)*
in case he starts with a ..... *(plötzlich)* jerk!"

CHARLES SCHULZ

Can you complete the line above?

***Exercise 3**

Translate.

1. Deine Antwort ist eindeutig *(clear)* falsch.
2. Ich möchte das ganz klarmachen: es ist unmöglich.
3. Sein Bericht über das Ereignis war sehr detailliert.
4. Er berichtete detailliert über das Ereignis.
5. Er blickte mich freundlich an.
6. Da war eine alte Dame, die sehr freundlich aussah.
7. Der Autor spricht direkt zu seinen Lesern.
8. Dein Vorschlag klingt sehr unrealistisch.

***Exercise 4**

Put in the right adjective and/or adverb.

1. I wish I could speak English as .... *(good)* as James.
2. Besides James is one of the .... *(interesting)* people I've ever met.
3. Jill doesn't speak as .... *(good)* as James, but her written work is much .... *(good)* than his.

4. English is an .... *(easy)* and .... *(convenient)* language to learn but you can pick up American English even .... *(easy)* than British English.
5. Your friend Tom speaks English .... *(careful)* than you do; he is one of the .... *(careful)* users of the language that I know.
6. "Your English is .... *(bad)* this year than it was last year." – "Sorry, I've had a .... *(bad)* teacher recently; his English is .... *(good)* than that of some of his students."

***Exercise 5**

Translate. Are you sure whether to use an adjective or on adverb?

a)

1. Im allgemeinen ist der Mensch ein geselliges Wesen.
2. Das ist allgemein zutreffend.
3. Allgemeinc Wahlen finden alle vier Jahre statt.
4. Diese Tatsache ist allgemein akzeptiert.
5. Im allgemeinen stehe ich um 6:30 auf.
6. Hoffentlich wird sich alles ändern.
7. Kannst du einen knappen Bericht vom Treffen geben?
8. Kurz gesagt, das Treffen fand nicht statt.
9. Wir werden wahrscheinlich wieder hinfahren müssen.
10. Dieser Ausgang der Sache ist sehr wahrscheinlich.

b)

1. Was du sagst, ist einfach falsch.
2. Sie schreibt in einem klaren und einfachen Stil.
3. Sag es so einfach, wie du kannst.
4. Der Text ist extrem schwierig zu verstehen.
5. Er vertritt eine extrem unterschiedliche Auffassung.
6. Es gibt extreme Unterschiede in ihren Auffassungen.
7. Der Autor beschreibt das Haus detailliert.

8. Ab Zeile 21 wird er sehr detailliert.
9. Allgemein gilt das als altmodisch.
10. Die Frage ist von allgemeinem Interesse.
11. Das ist ironisch gemeint.
12. Der Titel ist klar ironisch.

Verbs: General

Exercise 1

Noun and verb must agree.

1. Her aunt and uncle .... *(have)* a small cottage in Cornwall.
2. My father .... *(have)* a well-paid job.
3. There .... *(have)* been a lot of noise in our neighbours' flat recently.
4. There .... *(happen)* a lot of crimes every day.
5. 42.2 km .... *(be)* a long distance to run without a pause.
6. Over 500 people .... *(be)* the largest number known to have died in a single plane crash.
7. Apple-pie and custard .... *(be)* a typical British dessert.
8. Bad news .... *(be)* good news, newspapermen .... *(say)*.

Exercise 2

Check the irregular verbs and spot the mistakes.
(Some sentences are correct.)

1. This text can be understand as a warning against the arms race.
2. Our attention is catched by the gruesome facts about war reality.
3. The author chose his words very carefully.
4. I've heard that you believe the Star Wars programme will be the solution.
5. Have you went out of your mind? I would have thought you were more sensible.

6. It was a risk but, fortunately it has payed off.
7. In his article the author has showed us which way to take in the years to come.

Exercise 3

Check the form of the verbs.

1. The text is about the problems this school faces with.
2. Less bright students are sent to classes where basic English are taught.
3. Taken everything into consideration one must favour 'streamed' classes.
4. Nobody need to feel inferior when they are sent down to level 'C'.
5. Success at school not only depends on one's intelligence alone.
6. You can only wait how things develops in the future.
7. The unexpected date with his former girl-friend made his brain working.
8. He can not imagine what makes him so attractive to her.
9. He realised that they didn't have seen each other for ages.
10. In the meantime he had heared about her promising career in New York.
11. He noticed the smile on her face but he did not know what that was meaning.
12. He was not been in that town for about twenty years.
13. The hotelboy offered to help carry his bags; he said he could it himself.

***Exercise 4**

Check the nouns/verbs and spot the mistakes. (Some sentences are correct.)

1. The mass media is responsible for the growing violence in our streets.
2. Many newspapers and magazines run articles on educational problems.
3. There happens a lot of incredible things every day.
4. The 'News of the World' are one of the papers I'll never read.
5. Bad news is often good news for journalists.
6. Newspapermen do not always tell the truth.
7. One of the British delegates speak excellent German.

***Exercise 5**

Tick which of these verbs can be used in sentence a), b) or c).

admit	confess	persuade	say
affirm	convince	point out	state
assert	explain	promise	suggest
assure	inform	remark	tell
believe	mention	report	warn

a) He said that we would get into trouble.
b) He told me that we shouldn't/wouldn't get there in time.
c) He explained to me that he would come, too.

"This one ..... it's overpriced."

Put in a suitable verb from the list above.

***Exercise 6**

Complete these sentences in any suitable way.

1. Mother suggested ...
2. Father advised ...
3. My younger sister insisted ...
4. Father persuaded ...
5. I myself disapproved ...
6. I rather wanted ...
7. Then my father mentioned ...
8. Mother warned ...
9. She explained ...
10. Father assured ...
11. I told ...
12. My sister said ...

* Revision

Check the verbs and spot the mistakes.

1. The author wants to make them clear that they canot sit back and wait.
2. An unpleasant smell made us leaving the room at once.
3. The judge wanted that the young man plead guilty.
4. The young man, who thought to have the right to speak, protested loudly.
5. Arriving at home the quarrel with his parents began.
6. The father said his son to keep quiet.
7. That was the moment the son had been waited for. He slammed the door and was off.
8. A wide issue in the U.K. these days are the growing number of people who are crazy about guns.
9. The Government trys to develop new guidelines on gun control.
10. So far the British don't be afraid of walking in the streets at night.
11. Citizens without a serious reason aren't be allowed to own firearms.
12. In the streets of London you are used to see officers ("Bobbies") who do not carry guns.
13. Any type of gun from the most simple to the most sophisticated is send by mail order if you want so.
14. The solution to this issue? It not depends on the policy of the government alone.
15. The main reason for the alarming increase of violence are the 1 mio licensed guns in private hands.

Verbs: Tenses

*Exercise 1

a) *Which is the correct tense: past or past perfect?*

1. We .... *(meet)* John in town yesterday.
2. What he .... *(say)*?
3. He .... *(say)* that he .... *(be)* ill for almost six weeks but he .... *(be)* better in the meantime.
4. He .... *(tell)* us that his boss .... *(worry)* when and where John .... *(contract)* that illness.
5. John .... *(add)* that he .... *(be)* only too glad that he .... *(recover)* after four weeks of lying in bed.
6. In his summer vacation John .... *(be)* to the Fiji Islands; perhaps he .... *(infect)* himself there.
7. We .... *(tell)* John that we .... *(miss)* him at our Friday parties and that many friends .... *(ask)* about his whereabouts.
8. We .... *(not be)* in the position to tell them what .... *(happen)* to John.

b) *Translate. Which is the correct tense: past or present perfect?*

1. Thomas ist in England gewesen. Dort hat er sein Englisch gelernt.
2. Letzte Woche habe ich den neuen Science-fiction-Film gesehen.
3. Unsere Freunde leben seit vier Jahren in den USA. Sie sind im Jahre 1986 dorthin gegangen.
4. Er wartet schon seit einer Stunde auf sie. Er steht hier schon seit 7 Uhr.
5. Sie ist gegangen, weil sie rechtzeitig zu Hause sein mußte.
6. Das Geld ist bereits letzte Woche bezahlt worden. Diese Woche haben wir noch nichts verdient.

7. Ich bin oft gefragt worden, ob ich England oder die USA vorziehe. Ich habe nie darüber nachgedacht.
8. Ich habe den Unterschied zwischen dem „Past“ und dem „Present Perfect“ noch nicht verstanden.

***Exercise 2**

Which of the future forms a) – f) fit(s) the following sentences? (There may be more than one solution in most sentences!)

a) will-future
b) going to + infinitive
c) present continuous
d) future continuous
e) simple present
f) be about to + infinitive

1. Most areas .... *(be)* sunny tomorrow and we .... *(have)* intermittent showers in many places.
2. We .... *(find)* a cure for Aids but in the meantime this disease .... *(claim)* thousands of victims a year.
3. If you .... *(live)* in the city, you .... *(suffer)* from noise pollution.
4. A) The professor .... *(be)* busy I'm afraid. He .... *(give)* two lectures in the morning and another one in the afternoon.
   B) He .... *(leave)* by 5:30 in the morning.
   C) Oh, sorry, I see he .... *(leave)* now.
5. A) You .... *(get)* up or you .... *(stay)* in bed all Sunday?
   B) If you .... *(get)* up, don't go outside. It .... *(be)* very cold later in the day.
   C) You .... *(feel)* the low temperatures as soon as you .... *(go)* out.
6. A) By this time next year we .... *(travel)* through America.
   B) When you .... *(go)* to the States you .... *(meet)* a lot of friendly people.
   C) When you .... *(book)* your flight ticket?
   D) I have already booked my flight. My plane .... *(leave)* at 7:30 from Frankfurt next Sunday.

*Exercise 3

Check the conditional clauses and spot the mistakes.

1. What would you do if somebody would give you a flight ticket?
2. If my father didn't allowed me to fly, I'd have to stay in Germany.
3. If the traffic hadn't been so heavy, we had reached the airport in time.
4. If you'll tell me why you're worried, I can try to help you.
5. It would be much better if children can do what they want.
6. She were come if you had asked her to come.
7. If you had told us everything, we would been informed.
8. They had agreed if we had been a little more polite.

*Exercise 4

Translate. Keep special attention to the conditionals.

1. Wenn ich jünger wäre, würde ich Fremdsprachen studieren.
2. Ich würde Lehrer werden, wenn diese besser bezahlt würden.
3. Ich hätte meine Studien nicht begonnen, wenn ich gewußt hätte, daß sie so lange dauern.
4. Ich würde das nicht sagen, wenn ich es nicht wüßte.
5. Wenn Sie in unserer Firma erfolgreich sein wollen, müssen Sie hart arbeiten.
6. Sie wären sicher gekommen, wenn wir sie eingeladen hätten.
7. Wenn das stimmte, würden wir nicht widersprechen.

*Exercise 5

Meet some old friends: conditionals.

1. If I were more fortunate, I .... *(certainly make it).*
2. I would certainly have made it if I .... *(more fortunate).*
3. If I ever pass that test, I .... *(be most fortunate).*
4. Should I be as fortunate with my test as you have been, I .... *(ring you up)* to let you know.

5. Why don't you object if you .... *(not agree)*?
6. If I .... *(be)* you, I would stand up and protest at once.
7. I would have protested if .... *(be treated)* like you have been for years by this company.
8. If you don't speak up for your right, they .... *(simply forget)* you.

"Protocol or no, if he ..... *(not stop)* talking, I ..... *(eat)* him."

** **Exercise 6**

Join each sentence pair by forming a conditional *(a) or a* concessive *(b)* clause.

a) if, unless, in case, supposing that
b) although, despite the fact that, in spite of

1. Look through my binoculars. You can see the mountain tops clearly.
2. Look that way. Otherwise you won't see anything.
3. We took the binoculars. But we couldn't see anything.
4. I had the best pair of binoculars in the world. Still I couldn't see much. (It was too hazy).
5. I'll let you go home on one condition. You'll have to leave in silence.

6. We tried to leave the building in complete silence. Yet we did not pass unnoticed.
7. You'd better leave now. Otherwise it might be too late.
8. You want to leave early tomorrow? Then let me know this evening.
9. I have no idea so far what we can do about it. But we'll find a way.
10. In the beginning her fears were enormous. She overcame them in the end.

Verbs: Passive Voice

Exercise 1

Transform into the passive.

1. People build more and more high-rise blocks.
2. They have never accepted him as he was.
3. One can easily understand his fears.
4. They tried and condemned the kidnapper.
5. I've heard they are building the new sports arena next to the old one.
6. People say he is something of an outsider.

*Exercise 2

Translate into the passive.

1. Uns wurde ein Film über England gezeigt.
2. Man kümmerte sich um den alten Mann.
3. Für meine Idee wurde mir eine extra Prämie gegeben.
4. Man geht davon aus, daß du für den Job geeignet bist.
5. Man glaubt, er wird es schaffen.
6. Niemand hatte je von einer solchen Sensation gehört.
7. Das Essen wurde von Vater bezahlt.
8. Ist dir schon eine Lehrstelle angeboten worden?

*Exercise 3

Is the passive correct? Spot the mistakes.

1. English is spoken by stewardesses all over the world.
2. The plane was not been checked carefully before the flight.
3. Do you know what is to do before the plane takes off?
4. The new airport was build five years ago.
5. Before the start seat-belts have to be fastened.
6. Drinks aren't be served before take-off.
7. "Our passengers are invited to have a glass of champagne today."
8. "Our flight was great: we have be invite to a glass of champagne."

*Exercise 4

Translate and give special attention to verb forms.

1. Er war gekommen, um das Topspiel zu sehen.
2. Das Spiel war unglücklicherweise abgesagt worden.
3. Er hätte es wirklich gern gesehen.
4. Aber da war im Augenblick nichts zu machen.
5. Das mußte nun akzeptiert werden.
6. Das nächste Mal würden die Mannschaften erst vierzehn Tage später aufeinandertreffen.
7. Er hoffte, daß er in zwei Wochen nicht wieder enttäuscht würde.
8. Er hatte sich seit einem Monat auf dieses Topspiel gefreut.

Verbs: ing-Form vs. Infinitive

Exercise 1

Which is correct: ing-form or infinitive?

1. I want everyone .... *(listen)* to this.
2. Most people like .... *(drive)* better than .... *(walk)*.
3. I'd like .... *(buy)* that camera; it's a bargain.

4. My friends enjoy .... *(go)* to a discotheque on Friday nights.
5. I'm looking forward to .... *(go)* to the pop concert next week.
6. I should advise you .... *(see)* a doctor. You don't look well.
7. My parents expect me .... *(be)* back by 11 o'clock.
8. Do you mind .... *(give)* me a hand? It's too heavy.
9. As the last bus had gone, he suggested .... *(take)* a taxi.
10. The teacher made him .... *(repeat)* the entire sentence.
11. The sergeant ordered his men .... *(get)* moving.
12. .... *(See)* his former girlfriend .... *(come)* towards him, he wanted .... *(avoid)* .... *(say)* 'hello' to her.

ORLANDO BUSINO

"It started with him simply bringing me my slippers at home."

***Exercise 2**

ing-form or infinitive in the passive?

1. I would like .... *(ask)* before my personal things are used.
2. Children all over the world like .... *(read)* to.
3. I don't mind .... *(make)* fun of.
4. Nobody wants .... *(wake)* up in the middle of the night; everybody prefers .... *(leave)* in peace when they sleep.

5. Fruit should .... *(wash)* and/or .... *(peel)* before it can .... *(consume)*.
6. I love .... *(invite)* to dinner in an expensive restaurant, but tonight I should hate .... *(invite)*: there is football on TV.
7. He couldn't avoid .... *(address)* wherever he went.
8. We are looking forward to .... *(receive)* by our mayor next week.

***Exercise 3**

Complete the following sentences.

1. I used to .... *(travel)* a lot when I was younger.
2. He is not used to .... *(live)* in the city.
3. You have to get used to .... *(speak)* in front of the class.
4. My father used to .... *(walk)* long hours; he hates cars.
5. I'm not used to .... *(be)* told what I have to do.
6. The writer used to .... *(work)* during the night; he suffered from insomnia.

Miscellaneous

Exercise 1

as or **than**

1. The only woman on the committee appeared more competent .... all her male colleagues.
2. She was willing to accept other opinions .... her own.
3. The male colleagues were less respected .... she was.

"I'm a hell of a lot more endangered ..... you are!"

4. No sooner did she stand up to speak .... the audience became silent.
5. As a speaker she was more persuasive .... most of her colleagues.
6. Her statements are in fact considered less boring .... those of her male counterparts.

*Exercise 2

Translate into English.

1. Sie waren zu spät, oder?
2. Du bist noch nicht in den USA gewesen, nicht wahr?
3. Ihr geht oft ins Kino, nicht?
4. Du verstehst schon, was ich sage, oder?
5. Du sahst, was passiert ist, nicht?
6. In der Arbeit ist kein Fehler gewesen, oder?
7. Er mag Musik, nicht wahr?
8. Du kannst nicht eventuell kommen, oder?

*Exercise 3

Translate into English. Keep special attention to German 'lassen'.

let us ...	= einen Vorschlag machen
let s.b. do s.th.	= jemandem etwas erlauben
to leave s.b./s.th.	= jemanden/etwas zurücklassen; jemanden/etwas sich selbst überlassen
to have s.b. do s.th. to make s.b. do s.th.	= jemanden veranlassen, etwas zu tun
to have s.th. done	= etwas erledigen lassen

1. Laßt uns darüber reden.
2. Er ließ die Schüler viele Vokabeln lernen.
3. Der Unfallflüchtige ließ den Verletzten auf der Straße liegen.
4. Meine Eltern lassen mich fernsehen, soviel ich will.

5. Der Zollbeamte läßt uns sämtliche Koffer öffnen.
6. Laß uns in Ruhe!
7. Er ließ seinen Wagen waschen.
8. Was hat dich deine Meinung so schnell ändern lassen?
9. Sie ließ den Motor laufen. Sie wollte nur den Brief einwerfen.
10. Lassen Sie sich Zeit.
11. Der Arzt ließ den Patienten ins Krankenhaus bringen.
12. Er ließ uns eher nach Hause gehen.

"Let's all wait for an open convertible."

**Exercise 4

Translate into English. Keep an eye on German 'sollen'. There may be more than one solution in some sentences.

man sollte eigentlich	=	one ought to; should
es wird erwartet	=	to be expected/supposed to
wie man sagt	=	to be said/reported to
Möchtest du, daß ... ?	=	Shall ... ?
dahinterstehende Absicht	=	to be meant/intended to

1. Man sollte die Wahrheit sagen.
2. Er soll ein berühmter Mann gewesen sein.
3. Sollen wir heute etwas später kommen?
4. Der Text soll ausdrücken, was ich denke.
5. Ihr sollt die „papers" gut aufheben und von Zeit zu Zeit wiederholen.
6. Was soll das bedeuten?

7. Der Leser soll aufgestachelt werden.
8. Der Arzt soll sofort kommen.
9. Sie soll als Fotomodell für ‚Vogue' arbeiten.
10. Ich sollte eigentlich heute abend meine Eltern anrufen.

**Exercise 5

Complete the following sentences. Give special attention to German 'was'.

Bezug auf vorhergehenden Satz	=	which
Frage	=	what?
		that which / everything that } what

JOHN CALDWELL

1. .... are you doing in the middle of the night?
2. That was exactly .... I had expected.
3. Briggs had the gun in his hand, ... seemed to make him a suspect.
4. Appleby asked Counterpoynt .... he was waiting for.
5. Briggs was innocent, ... was supported by Counterpoynt's confession.
6. At the very end of the story the reader is informed of .... has happened in the car.
7. Briggs had a sound alibi, ... proved he was innocent.

**Exercise 6

Translate the following sentences. Give special attention to German 'wie'.

Zahl, Grad, Maß	= how ...
welcher Art ...	= what ..... like
wie wär's mit ...	= what about ...
Name, Bezeichnung	= what ...
..., wie? (..., nicht wahr?)	= question tag
so wie ... (Vergleich)	= as ..... as
Apposition	= like

1. Wie alt bist du?
2. Wie heißt die englische Königin?
3. Wir sollten Menschen akzeptieren, wie sie sind.
4. Kein Geschäft ist wie das Showgeschäft.
5. Sag mir, wie sie in Wirklichkeit ist.
6. Fahrt so vorsichtig, wie ihr könnt.
7. Wie wär's mit Fernsehen?
8. Der Film gibt uns eine gute Vorstellung davon, wie New York ist.
9. Der Witz war gut, wie?
10. Er erzählte alles, wie es geschehen war.

Prepositions

Exercise 1

Get your prepositions right.

1. Betty went ..... *(in/into)* the living-room.
2. Standing ..... *(in/into)* the middle of the room, she looked ..... *(after/for)* her parents, whom she wanted to talk ..... *(about/to/over)*.
3. ..... *(On/At/Of)* the age of eighteen it was time for her to live ..... *(at/on/of)* her own.
4. Her parents were watching a soap opera ..... *(at/in/on)* TV.
5. She was not going to stay ..... *(at/in/by)* home and live ..... *(at/with/by)* her parents any longer. There was so much to find out about life.
6. She told them she would move out and stay ..... *(at/with/by)* her boy-friend .... *(in/at)* London for the next few months.
7. Her parents were interested ..... *(in/at)* the TV programme only, they were unwilling to listen ..... *(at/to)* their daughter.

JOHN JONIK

Exercise 2

Get your prepositions right.

1. Have you read this most interesting book ..... Anthony Burgess?
2. It is called '1985' and deals ..... educational and political problems of our time.
3. I am convinced ..... the fact that you may learn a lot ..... books.
4. Especially if they are written ..... competent authors.
5. ..... my mind '1985' is one of A. Burgess' best books.
6. He warns us ..... the growing power of trade unions.
7. Why don't you give '1985' a chance? We might discuss ..... some of its stimulating ideas in class.
8. Do you agree ..... me that reading books is rather important?

Exercise 3

Check the prepositions and spot the mistakes.

1. Have you ever heard of the novel 'The Catcher in the Rye' from J. D. Salinger?
2. The novel deals with an adolescent's disillusioning journey through New York.
3. Its hero, named Holden Caulfield, looks after people he can talk to.
4. He has left his school for good and does not want to stay by his parents. So he starts out on his own.
5. In all, he spends almost three days in New York's bars and hotels.
6. In opposite to the grown-ups he meets, Holden is a very sensitive young man.
7. At one time he dates 17-year-old Sally, a girl who is typical of a girl of her age.
8. Having read the book you will agree to me that it makes quite interesting reading.

***Exercise 4**

Translate and give special attention to prepositions.

1. die Geschichte von Conan Doyle
2. seine Haltung zu Verbrechen
3. Der Text erinnert mich an einen Film, den ich gesehen habe.
4. Sherlock Holmes sucht den Mörder.
5. Das Vergrößerungsglas ist charakteristisch für ihn.
6. Der Detektiv konzentriert sich auf das Motiv des Täters.
7. Erinnert ihr euch an 'The Hound of the Baskervilles'?
8. Glaubst du, daß Verbrecher vor ihrer Tat an die mögliche Strafe denken?

***Exercise 5**

Prepositions again: Pick the right one.

1. You object ..... *(with/to/of)* your opponent's view.
2. You reject ..... *(to/against/––)* an unfair proposition.
3. You faced ..... *(with/on/of)* a difficult situation.
4. You agree ..... *(with/––/to)* a standpoint you share.
5. You reflect ..... *(about/––/on)* the issue of democracy in the Third World.
6. You discuss ..... *(––/about/over)* this issue in class.
7. You react ..... *(on/to/at)* a provocation.
8. The author is concerned ..... *(about/with/––)* the topic of war.
9. Can you enlarge ..... *(––/about/on)* what you've just said?
10. Can you explain ..... *(to/––/in)* the class what you mean ..... *(with/by/of)* "weird"?

* Exercise 6

Check the prepositions and spot the mistakes.
(Several sentences are correct.)

1. '1984' is a novel from George Orwell.
2. The life depicted in that book is characteristic for a totalitarian regime.
3. In the aftermath of World War II Orwell was very concerned about our political future.
4. The world of 'Big Brother' provides a lot of examples for methods of terror practised there.
5. How do you react on what you read in that book?
6. In my view G. Orwell tries to warn us against the atrocities of totalitarianism.
7. In O'Brien's mind one has to fall in love with 'Big Brother' before one is able to integrate oneself in the society of '1984'.
8. Everything is controlled by the Party, proclaimed in the name of the Party and has to be in line with the Party ideology.

BILL WOODMAN

"..... course, right now it's only ..... and .....,
but we are working ..... the somersault."

somersault = *Salto*

Fill in the missing words.

*Exercise 7

Find the correct <u>*preposition*</u>*.*

text + **?**

1. the extract of a text ..... Charles Reich
2. That's a text ..... life in the 21st century.
3. This text is ..... considerable importance to us.
4. Let's take a closer look ..... the text.
5. The text consists ..... main clauses only.
6. It contains ..... few, if any, subclauses.
7. I'm going to prove this ..... the text.
8. That is typical ..... the text form called argumentative.
9. How do we approach ..... a non-fictional text?
10. The text divides ..... three sections.
11. Do you approve ..... the author's view in this text?
12. How is the film version *(verglichen mit)* ..... the original text?
13. Our text comes closer ..... expository text form.
14. In your "Kursarbeit" you'll be confronted ..... an unknown text.
15. What's your comment ..... this text?

*Exercise 8

of or **from**

1. We were on the road ..... London to Oxford.
2. In the collision one ..... my friends was badly injured. All ..... us were under shock.
3. ..... what I know the accident could not have been avoided.
4. Down at the hospital the doctor asked us where we came .....
5. That is some miles north ..... London, he said.
6. They had to keep our friend separated ..... the rest of us for a week or so.

7. They said they needed more information ..... us about the accident.
8. Always the same old story, they said. When there's fog on the roads, two out ..... three motorists drive too fast.

***Exercise 9**

Make sure you choose the right prepositions. Give special attention to German 'bei'.

räumliche Nähe	=	near; close to
wohnen bei ...	=	with (a person); at (s.b.'s place)
arbeiten bei ...	=	for
körperliche Berührung	=	by (the hand, etc.)
im übertragenen Sinn	=	with (children); in (a text)
zeitlich	=	at (sunrise)
wenn man ...	=	upon (... closer examination)

1. Das Abendessen bei unseren Freunden war sehr gut.
2. Bei mir ist das was anderes.
3. Bei Detektivgeschichten hängt viel von der Auflösung ab.
4. Wir kamen bei Sonnenuntergang an.
5. Bei näherem Hinsehen wird das klar.
6. In den Ferien waren wir bei Bordeaux.
7. Ich arbeite bei McDonald's.
8. Im Verkehr muß man bei älteren Leuten vorsichtig sein.
9. Ich kann bei meinen Freunden wohnen.
10. Sie nahm ihn bei der Hand.

***Exercise 10**

a) *Translate German 'für'.*

1. an example .....
2. a reason .....
3. a symbol .....
4. a proof .....

5. to be responsible .....
6. s.th. is typical .....
7. that is of considerable importance .....
8. this is characteristic .....
9. that is vital .....
10. important .....
11. a sign .....

b) **preposition** + **go(ing) home**

1. He tried to persuade her ....
2. He convinced me ....
3. He dissuaded her ....
4. He warned her ....
5. He advises her ....
6. He ordered them ....
7. He let them ....
8. He prevents them ....

*Exercise 11

How do you translate German 'durch'?

durch die Tür	=	through
im Passiv	=	by
mittels	=	by + ing-form; by means of; through
wegen; infolge von	=	owing to; because of; as a result of

1. Durch den Regen war die Straße unpassierbar.
2. Er sprang durch das Fenster.
3. Er beweist seine These durch Beispiele.
4. Amerika wurde durch die Wikinger entdeckt.
5. Durch seine Fahrweise hatten wir einen Unfall.
6. Der Mann wurde durch die Polizei verhaftet.
7. Durch einen Wechsel der Spur kamen wir in Gefahr.

**Exercise 12

Make sure of your prepositions.

1. *(angesichts)*
Man's helplessness ..... death is obvious.

2. *(durch)*
He illustrates his view .... facts and examples.

3. *(Bei)*
.... Shakespeare everything is different.

4. *(in Beziehung auf)*
The price of the house seems high .... what we earn.

5. *(Im Hinblick auf)*
.... the fact that everybody is broke we'd better forget about it.

6. *(Dank)*
.... their incredible luck all passengers survived the crash.

"Oh, by the way ... according to my teacher I'm suffering from a lack of discipline in the home. See to it, will you ...?"

**Exercise 13

Translate into English.

according to	due to	owing to
along with	except for	in comparison with
as for	in line with	in relation to
because of	by means of	in view of

1. Außer dem Schiedsrichter waren alle wütend.
2. Diese Entwicklung stimmt überein mit der neuesten Mode.

3. Im Hinblick auf die Tatsache, daß er vielleicht lügt, müssen wir sorgfältig zuhören.
4. Gemäß der Aussage des Arztes wurde er erschossen.
5. Die Löhne sind im Verhältnis zu den Lebenshaltungskosten niedrig.
6. Wir verpaßten den Flug infolge des Taxifahrerstreiks.
7. Ebenso wie tausend andere verließen wir die Gegend.
8. Bezüglich unserer Kursarbeit werde ich euch morgen informieren.
9. Der Kandidat gewann gegen seinen Rivalen mit Hilfe einer schmutzigen Kampagne.

*** Revision**

1. We are going to study the story 'Tell-tale Heart' ..... E.A. Poe.
2. Its narrative point of view is characteristic ..... a crime story.
3. What attitude does the narrator take ..... the crime he commits?
4. He makes me think ..... a true madman, obsessed ..... persecution mania.
5. As he describes his murderous act he appears proud ..... his accurate work.
6. The loud heartbeat is a sign ..... his madness.
7. Finally the police arrive to search ..... the old man reported missing.
8. ..... the point of view ..... the police the narrator is certainly mad.
9. Let's discuss ..... the question ..... his madness.
10. Can he be blamed ..... what he has done?
11. What is your reaction ..... the news?
12. You take an attitude ..... fear ..... a situation you are afraid ..... .
13. What is your outlook ..... life?
14. Have you any difficulty ..... speaking English?
15. Next week you'll hear a statement ..... the topic of the trade unions in Great Britain.
16. I hear you take a great interest ..... sports.
17. Did you discuss ..... the environmental situation of the Rhine?
18. If we look at it ..... this angle we can agree.

Vocabulary

General

Exercise 1

Make sure of your vocabulary.

1. *(typisch für)*
   The phrase "You are too young for that" is .... parents.
2. *(glücklich)*
   The parents tried everything they could to make their daughter ....
3. *(Meinung)*
   I've got a different .... , though.
4. *(Im Gegensatz zu)*
   .... members of the older generation many young people are idealistic.
5. *(gibt es)*
   Among the younger generation .... quite a few who say "I want to live now".
6. *(ihm klarmachen)*
   I must .... / .... what I think of people over thirty.

Exercise 2

Find a synonym (word or expression with a similar meaning).

1. Finally they agreed to come.
2. I'm sure we can handle that.
3. To my mind that's rubbish!
4. He is regarded as a good chap.
5. This becomes clear if you look at p. 3.
6. Can you give evidence from the text?
7. In our story there are two very different characters.
   They stand in a striking contrast to each other.

8. In the course of the story the possibility of a violent confrontation becomes bigger and bigger.
9. In the end the chance of such a confrontation gets smaller.
10. Both have the chance of changing their situation for the better.

Exercise 3

Spot the mistake.

a)

1. In opposite to the world around him he lives in a dream.
2. In the world of the grown-ups it gives no chance for him to survive.
3. The prove of this can be seen in the image of the "catcher in the rye".
4. When he meets Sally Hayes, he is fascinated by her outlook.
5. Their date is also not successful.
6. Sally argumentates like an adult would do.
(His name? Why, Holden Caulfield of course!)

b)

1. Paula's youth had been the baddest time of her life.
2. The old photos remembered her of her unfortunate school days.
3. She is old enough now: she is possible to stand on her own feet.
4. During you go to school, you needn't worry about a job.
5. Some people say growing-up means the step from innocent to guilt.
6. There is nearly no chance for you to take up the job you want.
7. More and more young people are desperated when they think of their future.

Exercise 4

Enlarge your vocabulary.

1. *(Einerseits ..... andererseits)*
.... pop stars earn a lot .... they must work hard for it.
2. *(beschreibt ..... detailliert)*
The author .... the pop concert ....

ELDON DEDINI

"Did you ever have a beautiful thought and you just couldn't find the words to express it?"

3. *(Während)*
.... pop stars are at the top, they must take their chances.

4. *(bekommen)*
Every talent should .... the chance to find what he or she can do.

5. *(hängt ab von)*
The band's success .... how the public will like their sound.

6. *(es macht ihm Spaß, zu)*
He told me .... playing the lead guitar.

7. *(bringt)*
To support his main idea the author ..../ .... a lot of well-known facts.

8. *(seine eigene Meinung)*
In the last part he expresses .... opinion as to the Star Wars programme.

9. *(spricht ..... direkt an)*
The author .... his readers ....

10. *(erreicht)*
I think the writer .... the effect intended.

11. *(reagiert auf)*
The way she .... his behaviour seems exaggerated.

12. *(ernst nehmen)*
We must .... that development ....

13. *(Individuum)*
Man is said to be an .... with basic needs and various interests.

14. *(monoton)*
Daily life can become very ....

15. *(soll)*
This article .... / .... to illustrate the problem of unemployment in our country.

*Exercise 5

Find a better version for the underlined words.

1. There are some good points about streamed classes.
2. The number of teacher students has gone down dramatically.
3. Mixed ability classes are formed to get no conflicts among students.
4. The author puts sentences together by means of 'and'.
5. That means he writes in main clauses only.
6. The text shall give the reader a clear idea of the class system in the U.K.
7. Most people work hard to get into a higher social position.
8. It is certainly not a good idea to build up a new class society.
9. The British Government wants to fight against these problems.
10. Serious problems may come up, if the nations of the world do not change their environmental policies.

Note: streamed = *leistungsdifferenziert*
mixed ability = *mit verschiedenen Leistungsniveaus*

*Exercise 6

Enlarge your vocabulary.

1. *(Zwar)*
   .... people say 'crime doesn't pay' but what about our crime rates?
2. *(möchte zeigen)*
   The author .... / .... that man's future is at stake.
3. *(sinnlos ..... sinnvoll)*
   Some say hard work in itself is .... while others claim it .... for one's individual development.
4. *(nicht optimal)*
   The solution that you propose is ....
5. *(machen)*
   Travelling abroad you can .... the most rewarding experiences.
6. *(eine eigene Meinung)*
   She definitely had ....

7. *(Mit ..... ist gemeint, daß)*
.... the word ‘self-conscious’ .... that you have little or no confidence.

8. *(Wenn ich mich recht erinnere)*
.... we will do a class test next week.

9. *(Es läßt sich nicht leugnen)*
.... that class tests mean hard work, don’t they?

10. *(Ich wage zu behaupten)*
.... that it pays to be well-prepared.

11. *(unter anderem)*
You’ll have to write, ... , a comment I’m afraid.

12. *(Abgesehen von)*
.... that comment there’ll be one or two questions on formal aspects of the text.

13. *(Daraus folgt, daß)*
.... you had better review some of our texts.

14. *(soll sein)*
Orwell’s ‘1984’ .... one of the most important novels written in our century.

15. *(totalitär)*
The book depicts a .... state.

16. *(Individuen)*
The citizens of ‘Oceania’ are no longer ....

17. *(sollen)*
They .... adjust to the one-party system in power.

18. *(wendet an)*
The regime of ‘1984’ .... oppressive methods.

19. *(unter)*
Hatred and suspicion are common .... the citizens.

20. *(will, daß)*
The official ideology .... the people .... distrust and betray each other.

*Exercise 7

Do you know these stock phrases? Translate.

1. if my memory serves me right
2. apart from that
3. as for me
4. among other things
5. I beg to disagree
6. what is indeed striking here is
7. it can be argued that
8. it is important to differentiate between
9. by the way
10. hence it follows that
11. if I may put it this way
12. there is no denying that
13. if I remember correctly
14. I dare say
15. apart from

*Exercise 8

Enlarge your vocabulary.

1. *(kommt mir ..... vor)*
   The way he behaves in the story .... unrealistic.
2. *(Während)*
   .... you go to the letter box you might empty the dustbin.
3. *(nahezu keine)*
   He has .... hope left to get a new job.
4. *(Wenn man alles in Betracht zieht)*
   .... I can fully understand what the author says.
5. *(Aus meiner Sicht)*
   .... that seems highly improbable.

6. *(engagierte sich für)*
   She .... / .... social work.
7. *(hat resigniert)*
   Seeing that it was hopeless he has ...../......
8. *(soll ausdrücken)*
   The image .... / .... the idea of man's loneliness.
9. *(läßt sich belegen)*
   This .... / .... in the last paragraph when the author says ...
10. *(sind)*
    In any school .... / .... more than enough people you do not care for.
11. *(erfuhren)*
    It was through him that we .... / .... about the school strike.
12. *(gekennzeichnet)*
    Their relationship is .... / .... by enmity and hatred.
13. *(ist zurückzuführen auf)*
    His shyness .... / .... his lack of self-confidence.
14. *(zugeben)*
    I'll have to .... / .... that my first impression was wrong.
15. *(heutzutage ..... damals)*
    Young people are much different .... from what they were ....

*Exercise 9

Spot the mistake in the following sentences.

1. There are much jobs available but they are underpaid.
2. You'll have to choice whether to accept one of these or not.
3. Before putting it on the market we must prove the new chemical in our labs.
4. Another point of critic is that the chemical industry is deaf to complaints.
5. The poet describes the scenery very detailed.
6. The factory owner lets other people work for him.
7. To me that is an example of unhuman behaviour.
8. There is a broad discussion going on about different conceptions of live.
9. Too many people die by the follows of our modern civilization.

10. It becomes aware that we cannot communicate successfully with each other.
11. No matter where we look we are surrounded by indifference and unpersonal behaviour.
12. It is paradox that people feel more and more lonely in the big cities.
13. In l. 25 the author brings a good argument.

*Exercise 10

Enlarge your vocabulary.

1. *(läßt sich belegen)*
   The protagonist's estrangement .... / .... in ll. 23–27.
2. *(wird deutlich)*
   The protagonist's estrangement .... in ll. 23–27.
3. *(lautet wie folgt)*
   His main thesis .... / ....
4. *(ist)*
   In the last part .... / .... a change of atmosphere.
5. *(Mit ..... ist gemeint, daß)*
   The word/image/sentence in l. 30 .... that his situation is not without hope.
6. *(Die Figur X steht im Mittelpunkt)*
   The story .... / .... the character of X.
7. *(spiegelt)*
   The "Bildzeitung" .... / .... the opinions of the 'man in the street'.
8. *(bildet)*
   The last part .... / .... the climax of the text.
9. *(ist voller)*
   The text passage .... / .... symbolic allusions.
10. *(ganz am)*
    The murder occurs at .... beginning; the solution is given at the .... end only.
11. *(dringend)*
    This is a very .... / .... problem indeed.
12. *(auffallend)*
    Another .... / .... feature is his impatience with other people.

13. *(sich bewußt werden)*
    The boy .... / .... his own weakness.
14. *(verhalten sich anders als)*
    Daughters and sons .... what parents expect.
15. *(Selbstverwirklichung)*
    Leaving home when you're 18 is an act of .... , or an attempt to ....
16. *(machen sich Sorgen)*
    Many parents .... / .... the future of their children.

****Exercise 11**

Find a synonym for the underlined word(s).

1. The article is supposed to illustrate the danger of political extremism.
2. Let's try and solve the conflict now.
3. That is certainly a complicated question.
4. He simply can't make it clear to us what he means.
5. Her unfriendliness is due to her lack of sensitivity.
6. You express your doubts very clearly.
7. The author uses pejorative language.
8. The protagonist's way of speaking sounds aggressive.
9. In sum, the author is clearly against that.
10. The long and short of it is that he won't be able to come.
11. The text is characterized by abstract vocabulary.
12. I can't agree. Your argument is ill-founded.
13. Well, I'm rather doubtful if that is correct.
14. He committed himself to the peace movement.
15. The demonstration has been sparked off by the bad housing situation in the area.
16. There can be no doubt that there is trouble ahead.

The spectator's comment runs:
"Hogan seems very ..... *(selbstbewußt).*"

**Exercise 12

Enlarge your vocabulary.

1. *(Leider)*
   .... I can't accept your proposition.
2. *(einwenden)*
   One may .... / .... that this is untrue.
3. *(ist zurückzuführen auf)*
   The sudden change .... / .... the new managing director.
4. *(kommt in)*
   The student .... another class.
5. *(gehört in)*
   This item .... another category.
6. *(Teufelskreis)*
   Our neighbours are caught in a ....

7. *(hat ihr Gutes)*
   A strict hierarchy has its ...., though.
8. *(Selbstbewußtsein)*
   Your .... / .... is not what it should be.
9. *(sich selbst verwirklichen)*
   She is apparently trying to .... / ....
10. *(Selbstüberschätzung)*
    I believe he suffers from .... / he has ....
11. *(ist selbstverständlich)*
    That is .... / That goes ....

****Exercise 13**

a) *Enlarge your vocabulary.*

1. die Klassenunterschiede in Großbritannien
2. sich innerlich überlegen fühlen
3. an einem Unterlegenheitsgefühl leiden
4. ein Ziel verfolgen
5. nach einer höheren sozialen Position streben
6. sich sozialen Konventionen unterwerfen
7. durch Klassenvorurteile diskriminiert werden
8. seine soziale Position verbessern
9. Klassenschranken überwinden
10. sozial benachteiligt sein

b) *Can you find an antonym (= word or expression opposed in meaning)?*

1. to be brought up in a favorable home environment
2. to be born into the upper classes
3. to be conscious of one's origin
4. to widen class barriers
5. to fall down the social ladder
6. to resist against the norms of society

7. to <u>struggle ambitiously for s.th.</u>
8. to marry <u>above one's rank</u>
9. to <u>feel superior</u> to s.b.
10. to <u>miss</u> the goal you have set for yourself

**Exercise 14

Enlarge your vocabulary.

1. *(selbstgefällig)*
   His good looks make him .... / ....
2. *(selbstlos)*
   For as long as I can remember my mum has always been .... / ....
3. *(Selbstwertgefühl)*
   A little compliment now and then is good for her .... / ....
4. *(Wirklichkeit werden)*
   He believes his idea/plan/dream will .... / .... one day.
5. *(von)*
   That is certainly not fair .... your parents.
6. *(Leistung bringen)*
   In our competitive society everyone is supposed to .... / ....
7. *(kreisen um)*
   His thoughts .... / .... money-making.
8. *(beruht auf)*
   Success .... / .... on talent, hard work, and, sometimes, luck.

**Exercise 15

Enlarge your vocabulary.

1. *(Behauptung)*
   I am going to discuss the author's .... / .... concerning violent demonstrations.
2. *(uns auseinandersetzen mit)*
   First we have to .... / .... the definition of 'capitalism'.
3. *(eindrucksvoll)*
   That is a very .... / .... appeal to justice on the author's part.

4. *(auffallend)*
   There is a .... / .... similarity between mother and daughter.

5. *(entspricht der Wirklichkeit)*
   His portrayal of England .... / ....

6. *(macht die Erfahrung)*
   Everyone .... / .... that life is not a game.

7. *(hält sich an)*
   The author .... / .... the facts about the affair.

8. *(umstritten)*
   The latest tax plan is a .... / .... one.

9. *(kontrastiert mit)*
   The author's view .... my own standpoint.

10. *(existiert nicht)*
    A foolproof method to produce good testpapers ....

11. *(konstatiert)*
    The author .... / .... that things are not what they should be like.

12. *(kritisiert an)*
    This is precisely what the author .... our way life.

13. *(trägt bei zu)*
    His choice of words .... / .... the provocative effect of the text.

14. *(bewirkt)*
    Affluence .... / .... boredom and weariness of life.

Word Formation

Exercise 1

a) *Add a prefix to express the opposite.*

1. .....able
2. .....possible
3. .....capable
4. .....happy
5. .....satisfied
6. .....normal
7. .....human
8. .....personal
9. .....complete
10. .....true

b) *Find the prefix to express the opposite.*

1. .....illusion
2. .....information
3. .....difference
4. .....sense
5. .....understanding
6. .....violence
7. .....satisfaction
8. .....experience
9. .....advantage
10. .....agreement

Exercise 2

Find the corresponding verb.

1. introduction
2. conclusion
3. interpretation
4. quotation
5. enumeration
6. argumentation
7. assumption
8. explanation
9. juxtaposition
10. solution

Exercise 3

Find the corresponding noun.

1. to argue with s.b.
2. to assume s.th.
3. to solve a problem
4. to explain s.th. to s.b.
5. to prove s.th.
6. to indicate that ...
7. to criticize s.b.
8. to influence s.b.
9. to refer to s.th./s.b.
10. to infer s.th./that ...

Exercise 4

Think of word families to complete these sentences.

1. *(portrait)*
   The author .... life on a farm in England.
2. *(life)*
   He has .... on a farm for some years.
3. *(advice)*
   He .... the reader to keep his/her eyes open.
4. *(experiment)*
   The new machine is still in the .... stage.

5. *(add)*
   In .... to that we can observe many relative clauses.
6. *(to base)*
   What is the .... of our lives?
7. *(success)*
   I haven't seen you for five .... days.
8. *(intention)*
   Did you do that .... ? -- No, it was quite ....

Exercise 5

Add the right suffix(es).

a) -hood -ship -dom -ism -ation -ment -ness -ity -ion

friend..... star..... child..... glad..... ideal..... member.....
arrange..... consider..... adult..... capital..... dictator.....
king..... astonish..... implic..... christian..... weak.....
disappoint..... rela..... man..... critic..... confront.....
collect..... assumpt..... advertise..... partner..... free.....
material..... excite..... kind.....

b) -al -ive -(i)an -able -ible -ful -less -ous -like -y

(un)accept..... child..... sense..... peace.....
(un)communicat..... liter..... spontane..... figurat.....
meaning..... danger..... (in)visi..... habitu..... (un)change.....
(ir)respons..... Elizabeth..... cap..... (in)act..... usu.....
Victor..... harm..... (ir)reli..... persuas..... Georg.....
dream..... use..... length..... business..... mechanic.....

False Friends

Exercise 1

a) meaning or opinion

1. The word 'cry' has a double ....
2. Tell me your .... of British football and its supporters.
3. I don't understand the .... of this text.
4. The literal .... of 'symbol' is sign.
5. Does the newspaper article contain fact or .... ?
6. ....s were divided in the class.
7. What is the .... of all that noise outside?
8. I share your .... in every way.

b) remember or remind

1. Let me just .... you: it's 8:30, time to leave.
2. That music .... me of the Beatles.
3. You can still .... what you promised, can't you?
4. I .... we had a pretty cool summer last year.
5. That .... me: I must tell you about Peter.
6. Will you .... to drop me a card while you're in London?
7. Why didn't you .... me to post your letter. Sorry about that.
8. .... to bring your text books tomorrow.

c) interested or interesting

1. Thanks for your offer, but I'm not ....
2. What's .... in our museum of modern art?
3. That is a highly .... topic, I believe.
4. Are you .... in getting more information on this topic?

5. What you say sounds ....
6. He looked as if he wasn't .... in the topic we discussed.
7. My friend sounded .... (!) for once; he was speaking about his favourite topic: girls.

False Friends

d) **say** or **tell**

1. "What did you .... ?" – "I've never .... a word."
2. He .... me what you've .... him earlier.
3. We had enough of it, that is to .... , we were fed up with it.
4. He .... , "........ John what you've .... me."
5. Mother .... us that it is bad to .... a lie.
6. The teacher .... that everyone of us will have to .... one sentence about the text.
7. She .... that her little daughter can already .... the time.

e) **do** or **make**

1. We have .... all the homework we have been assigned.
2. I must have a new dress ....
3. You'll have to .... all the exercises I'm afraid.
4. What you say does not .... sense.
5. You should not say one thing and .... something else.
6. Let me just show you: I happen to know how that is ....
7. They .... him captain of his team.
8. What is Peter .... for a living?
9. Can you .... that for me?
   Can you .... it till 11h?

***Exercise 2**

a) **leave** or **let**

1. .... me help you.
2. You should .... her alone.
3. Why don't you .... it go at that?
4. Don't .... me down, will you?
5. He .... drop a remark.
6. He .... himself go.
7. You can .... the decision to your parents.
8. You .... the house in disorder.
9. ....'s .... it at that for the moment.

b) **new** or **news**

1. Radio announcer: It is 8:00. Here is the ....
2. That's a .... turn in the hostage drama.
3. What's the latest .... ?

4. One *(Nachricht)* .... runs that the Israeli hostages stand a chance of being released soon.
5. At the press conference there were some .... faces.
6. The PM came clean with the bad .... first.
7. What's .... in the .... ?

"Bad ....., Partridge – the computers can sell themselves now."

***Exercise 3**

see – look – watch

1. Kannst du verstehen, was ich meine?
2. Siehst du oft ‚Seifenopern'?
3. Egal wie du es siehst, es ist hoffnungslos.
4. Sieh mal dorthin: was kannst du sehen?

Find a good line for this cartoon using the verbs 'look – see – or watch'.

5. Ich wollte wegsehen, aber ich konnte nicht umhin, den Unfall anzusehen.
6. Hast du den Film gesehen, in dem der Junge immer Vögel beobachtet?
7. Wenn ich auf meine Kindheit zurücksehe, sehe ich, daß das Sehen der ‚Sesame Street' nicht nützlich war.

*Exercise 4

Beware of false friends!

1. *(rise vs. raise)*

   You needn't .... your voice nor need you .... to your feet if you feel like ....ing protest about the new high-........ blocks in our area.

2. *(topical vs. actual)*

   What was the .... result of that highly .... discussion we had? This book isn't .... anymore, is it? It has little value.

3. *(ready vs. finished)*

   Sorry, I haven't .... yet but in a minute I'll be .... to leave with you. Are you .... to begin after having .... your preparations?

4. *(nearly vs. hardly any)*

   There was .... hope left although I rang up .... all my friends some of whom I see .... more because there's .... always so much to do.

5. *(at last vs. at least)*

   You should .... try to work for the 'Kursarbeit' even if you fail .... So you will .... have no bad conscience when they announce the results ....

6. *(affect vs. effect)*

   What's the .... of the text on you? Has it .... you in some way at least? I hope it won't .... you in a negative way, otherwise our readings have produced a counter-.........

7. *(excited/exciting)*

   We were all very .... when we thought of the .... trip to China.

8. *(hard/hardly)*

   It was .... surprising that the boss expected us to work ....

9. *(except/accept)*

   When the teacher asked us, all .... one ....ed the proposition he made.

10. *(who's/whose)*

    .... in charge here? I wonder .... coat this is.

11. *(involved/engaged)*

    My brother has become .... with Greenpeace. My sister has no time for such things; she is .... with Robert.

12. *(realize/put in practice)*

    We had to .... that his plan was extremely difficult to ....

13. *(lie/lay)*

    I was .... in bed when the doctor .... the prescription on the bedside table, where it .... until my mother got the medicine.

14. *(adapt/adopt)*

    When he was .... by the Miller family he had to .... to their way of life.

15. *(fewer/less)*

    He worked .... hours and, consequently, he got .... pay, which he liked .... and ....

16. *(eventually/possibly)*

    When he .... called me he said he would .... get the new job.

17. *(sensible/sensitive)*

    She was a .... girl who held .... views on most issues.

18. *(self-conscious/self-confident)*

As he is rather ...., he should learn to become more ....

19. *(lose/loose)*

Are you going to set your dog ....? Aren't you afraid of .... him?

20. *(fly/flee)*

The only way for the runaway prisoner to .... was to .... to South America.

21. *(economic/economical)*

Are you satisfied with our .... system? My daughter is a very .... housewife.

22. *(human/humane)*

The fact that we belong to the .... race does not mean we are always ....

23. *(critic/criticism)*

This time the .... of the Trade Unions has gone too far in his ....

24. *(sympathetic/nice)*

He is a .... fellow. Besides he was very .... to me when I was down last year.

**Exercise 5

Translate and beware of false friends.

1. Ich möchte dir einen guten Rat geben.
2. Bevor er ging, gab er seinem Freund einige nützliche Ratschläge.
3. Ich erwarte keinerlei Ratschläge, ich muß mir selbst helfen.
4. Wir erhielten eine Menge wichtiger Informationen.
5. Können Sie mir Informationen über das englische Schulsystem geben?

** Exercise 6

Translate and give special attention to singular/plural of nouns.

1. Politik ist eine schwierige Materie.
2. Politiker wählen die Leute in ihrer unmittelbaren Umgebung sorgfältig aus.
3. Welche Informationen und faktischen Beweise lassen sich für die These des Präsidenten anführen?
4. Die Zuschauer sind sehr daran interessiert, dies aus den Massenmedien zu erfahren.
5. Demonstrationen sind ein friedliches Mittel des Protestes.
6. Nach mehreren Krisen erzielten die USA gute Fortschritte in ihren Verhandlungen mit der UdSSR.

* Revision

a) *Translate the following sentences.*

1. She is a most sympathetic person.
2. If he is too much under pressure, he may eventually break down.
3. Germany has the English side beaten.
4. He is the most ordinary chap I know.
5. Have you ever met someone more self-conscious than my friend?
6. Everybody says she is a very sensible girl.

b) *Watch out for false friends.*

1. *(Platz nehmen)*
   The host asked us to ....
2. *(stattfinden)*
   The exhibition match is scheduled to .... tonight.
3. *(auch keine)*
   What you suggest is .... solution ....
4. *(genial)*
   He was an .... / .... scientist.

5. *(familiäre)*
   The author employs .... language.
6. *(sinnvoll)*
   That (is) .... / .... in this context.
7. *(aufgezeigt werden)*
   This can be .... / .... in the opening scene of the play.

c) *Translate and beware of false friends.*

1. Er hat keine eigene Meinung.
2. Im Gegensatz zu mir hast du einen Job.
3. Wir denken, daß dieser Tag euch glücklich machen wird.
4. Es gibt keinen entscheidenden Unterschied.
5. Ich möchte den Grund dafür ausführlich erläutern.
6. Ihre Lebensumstände sind einfach unmenschlich.
7. Du bekommst dein Geschenk schon heute.
8. Der Text läßt sich in drei Hauptabschnitte unterteilen.
9. Die Anzeige soll die Haltung der Konsumenten beeinflussen.
10. Der Text erinnert mich an einen Film, den ich gesehen habe.
11. Im einführenden Teil stellt er sein Thema vor.
12. Im Hauptteil bringt er viele Fakten.
13. Das ist typisch für dich: niemals etwas zugeben!
14. Der Autor argumentiert einseitig.
15. Der Autor argumentiert konsequent.

Text Analysis and Text Production

Exercise 1

How to refer to a text: Translate into German.

1. A striking example of ... occurs in l. 20.
2. In ll. 31–35 the author points out that ...
3. That is revealed in ll. 45–47 when the author refers to ...

4. The word/sentence "..." in l. 20 suggests that ...
5. That can be traced in ll. 55–60.
6. Evidence of that/of ... is to be found in ll. 89–90.

Exercise 2

Find a synonym.

1. The story divides into three parts.
2. The main part covers ll. 15–70.
3. The last section reaches from ... to ...
4. To begin with the author introduces the theme.
5. The last unit contains the climax of the story.
6. The reader finally realizes the author's intention.

Exercise 3

Find a synonym for the underlined word/phrase.

1. The author writes about the environmental crisis.
2. In his latest book the reader is confronted with a rather pessimistic scenario.
3. The environmental question gets a particular significance.
4. The author lays stress on the necessity to act now.
5. Our present inactivity will most certainly lead to disaster.
6. Air pollution in particular causes health problems.
7. The author wants to say that ...
8. Can you give a satisfactory answer to the hunger problem in the world?
9. The author means that it is 5 to 12.
10. The writer wants to show that ...
11. He writes about environmental problems.
12. The text is full of images.
13. The author takes few compound sentences.
14. He does not give any value judgment but remains objective.

*Exercise 4

Enlarge your vocabulary of text analysis: Translate.

a) statement

The	author writer speaker	states asserts maintains affirms assumes implies points concludes infers	that …	
		tries to	show … prove … convince the reader.	

b) structure

The	author writer speaker	develops … organizes … arranges … compares … contrasts … juxtaposes … sets apart … draws an analogy between …

c) neutral attitude

The author	tries to be objective about … takes a neutral attitude towards … does not side with …

d) **positive attitude**

The author / writer / speaker
- defends the argument that ...
- is convinced of the fact that ...
- supports the idea of ...
- approves of the fact that ...
- underscores the idea that ...
- favours the view that ...
- is enthusiastic about ...

e) **argument**

He
- criticizes that ...
- attacks the idea that ...
- questions the facts about ...
- ridicules the idea of ...
- warns of a development that ... might/could ...
- does not take seriously ...
- expresses a doubtful view about ...
- speaks in an exaggerated way about ...

****Exercise 5**

Enlarge your vocabulary.

1. *(wird konkret)*
   In the middle part the author .... / ....
2. *(bleibt abstrakt)*
   From the very first line the author .... / ....
3. *(macht konkrete Angaben)*
   The author .... / .... on the job situation in the U.K.
4. *(Konkret gesprochen)*
   .... / .... that is absolutely impossible.
5. *(wie z. B.)*
   Birds, ... / .... eagles or falcons are considered noble.
6. *(bringt)*
   The author .... / .... / .... quite a few examples to support his view.

7. *(Wenn man z. B. ... nimmt)*
   ...., ... / ...., you must admit that I am right.

8. *(Weitere Beispiele für)*
   .... his attitude are to be found in ll. 32–37.

**Exercise 6

The words „good“ or „bad“ are not used in character analysis: Improve your vocabulary.

Complete and translate into German.

	optimistic		....	
	bright		....	
	law-abiding		disobedient	
	....		selfish	
	assertive		....	
	....		weak-willed	
	....		self-complacent	
	reliable		....	
	dynamic		....	
	regardful		....	
	....		intolerant	
a(n)	....	person is different from a(n)	inconsiderate	person
	....		depressed	
	sympathetic		....	
	sociable		....	
	grateful		....	
	conscientious		superficial	
	....		suspicious	
	....		aloof	
	tough		....	
	tactful		....	
	broad-minded		....	
	self-centred		....	
	....		responsible	

** Exercise 7

Vocabulary of text analysis: Translate.

a) effect on the reader

1. The author draws/focuses the reader's attention to/on ...
2. The author appeals to/plays on the reader's emotions.
3. The author stirs/arouses the reader's interest/imagination/fear, etc.
4. The author tries to/attempts to/intends to shift/influence the reader's attitude in favour of ...
5. The text/argument calls forth/evokes a response of ... in the reader.

b) re-formulation

1. namely (abbreviated: viz.)
2. in other words
3. that is (abbreviated: i.e.)
4. Another way of putting it is ...
5. To put it more simply/exactly ...
6. or rather

Exercise 8

Enlarge your vocabulary of text composition.

1. *(kann unterteilt werden in)*
   This text .... / .... three main sections.
2. *(reicht von ... bis)*
   The first unit .... / .... (l. 22–l. 35).
3. *(fängt an ... endet)*
   The second part .... in l. 17 and .... in l. 41.
4. *(umfaßt)*
   The third and last part .... ll. 55–60.
5. *(Als erstes)*
   .... / .... the author introduces his main thesis.
6. *(fährt fort)*
   He then .... / .... to develop his ideas in a more detailed way.
7. *(enthält)*
   The last passage .... / .... the conclusion of everything that has been said so far.

Exercise 9

How do you deal with the composition of texts?
Translate and add these expressions to your active vocabulary.

a)

As a first step ...

the author	introduces gives names	his topic/thesis/main idea.

The author	begins by pointing out ... quotes ... (a generally accepted authority). rejects/refutes ... (the thesis/the view of ...).

b)

In the following ...

the author	expands/develops/elaborates his thoughts. organizes / arranges ... in main steps. goes into detail. enumerates/accumulates ... examples of ... restricts himself to ... contrasts/juxtaposes ... (points, arguments). weighs the pros and cons of ...

c)

Finally ...

the author	concludes ... (his line of thought). winds up by saying ... draws the conclusion by saying ... returns to the beginning by saying ... underscores/emphasizes the idea of/the thesis of ...

Exercise 10

Enlarge your vocabulary of argumentation: Translate.

It has often been said that ...
People say that ...
The author maintains that ...

Well, this is simply not true.
Well, he/she is clearly wrong about that.
Frankly speaking, that is rubbish!

For one thing it cannot be denied that ...
Firstly it stands to reason that ...
On the one hand, what puzzles me is ...

For another, he fails to see that ...
Secondly, he overlooks that ...

Besides, you must consider that/admit that ...
Thirdly, my own experience tells me that ...

So it seems to me that ...
All things considered ...
Taking everything into account I should think ...
I am rather on ...'s side when it comes to ...

Collocations

*Exercise 1

Which verb(s) fit(s) best?

1. We might .... the story into five sections.
2. You are .... things too seriously. Relax!
3. It seems quite difficult for us to .... our minds.
4. He used every means to .... his aims.
5. Could you .... the point now?
6. I am sure he is the man to .... that difficult situation.
7. She .... an attitude of defiance.
8. Hence it .... that we are right.
9. The question .... as to what can be done about it.

*Exercise 2

Complete these collocations (= words that go together regularly).

1. Daraus folgt, daß ...	Hence it ....
2. Soweit es mich betrifft ...	As far as I ....
3. Das heißt ...	That is ....
4. Wie mir scheint ...	As it .... to me ...
5. Darüber hinaus ...	What is ....
6. Als ein erster Schritt ...	As a first ....
7. Aus meinem Blickwinkel ...	From my point ....
8. Wenn man alles in Betracht zieht ...	Taking everything ....

**Exercise 3

Complete these collocations.

1. You .... / .... an argument in a discussion or debate.
2. You .... / .... a solution to a problem.
3. You .... / .... a convincing proof of s.th.
4. You .... / .... a good/bad/favourable ... influence on s.b.
5. You .... an inference or conclusion from s.th.
6. You .... an assumption as to/as regards s.th.
7. You .... / .... an explanation of/for s.th.
8. You .... / .... an attitude of ... towards s.th./s.b.

*Exercise 4

Complete.

1. Zusammenfassend ...	= In ....
2. Um es kurz zu machen ...	= To cut a .... short
3. Mit einem Wort ...	= .... a word
4. Im ganzen ...	= On the ....

5. Alles in allem ... = (All) in ....
6. Kurz gesagt ... = To put it in a ....
7. Wenn man alles zusammennimmt ... = All things ....

****Exercise 5**

Which verb(s) fit(s) best?

1. He .... a comparison between the U.K. and Germany.
2. The long democratic tradition in the U.K. ..../........ a good example for our country.
3. The British press .... the function of watchdogs.
4. The "Letters to the Editor" column .... / .... a public platform of discussion.
5. The British press .... / .... a lot of praise.
6. Sometimes the press .... / .... a difficult situation whether to keep back information or publish it.
7. Every journalist, I am sure, ... / .... frustrating experiences.

****Exercise 6**

Complete these collocations.

1. *(tief)*
   You are .... impressed by the author's idea.
2. *(glatt)*
   You ..... refuse what you can't accept.
3. *(vage)*
   The speaker hinted .... at the idea of a new war.
4. *(bitter)*
   You comment .... on a situation that frustrates you.
5. *(lebhaft)*
   You imagine a situation .... if you have a clear idea of it.
6. *(präzise)*
   You have to explain a complicated problem .... if you want everybody else to grasp it.

**Exercise 7

Enlarge your vocabulary.

1. *(von überragender)*
   Today's results are of .... / .... importance for our team.
2. *(von geringer)*
   For our adversaries, on the other hand, they are of .... / .... importance only.
3. *(sinnvoll)*
   That's a very .... / .... question to ask.
4. *(lebendig, anschaulich)*
   The poet gives us a .... description of his father.
5. *(eng, vertraut)*
   Here we have a very .... / .... relationship among the members of the group.
6. *(angespannt)*
   At home we can sense the .... / .... atmosphere.
7. *(gemeinsam)*
   A feature that both texts .... / .... is the ironic undertone.
8. *(anständig)*
   We are entitled to be treated ....ly / with ....

**Exercise 8

Which verb(s) fit(s) best?

1. You .... from a text to support your view.
2. You .... to a text for proof.
3. You .... a thesis saying that ...
4. You .... / .... the thesis that ...
5. The author .... on / .... his main thesis in the main part of his text.
6. You .... at / .... to the conclusion that ...
7. The author .... / .... / .... by saying ...
8. An author .... into detail/into particulars.
9. He .... a comparison between ...

10. The author .... / .... two very different (= opposed) things/aspects/ events, etc.
11. Somebody's view/idea/argument/thesis ..../ ....
12. His arguments .... conviction; they .... proof; there .... no flaws in it.
13. The author .... / .... of/ .... to examples/commonly known facts/ accepted authorities/common sense, etc. in order .... / .... his ideas.
14. He .... / .... a clear distinction between ...
15. A closer look .... / .... that "things are not what they seem".

****Exercise 9**

Collocations again! Find words that go together with each keyword.

1. I think that is a(n) (+) .... / (–) .... argument.
2. We can observe a(n) (+) .... / (–) .... contrast.
3. *(zeigen/verbergen)* You (+) .... / (–) .... feelings.
4. In a relaxed / strained atmosphere you feel (+) .... / (–) ....
5. An author describes s.th. (+) .... / (–) ....

****Exercise 10**

a) *Supply suitable nouns.*

1. you deliver ....
2. you raise ....
3. you advocate ....
4. you evolve ....
5. you put forward ....

b) *Find suitable verbs.*

1. you .... a(n) aim/goal
2. you .... the function of
3. you .... evidence from the text
4. you .... an ironical attitude towards s.th.
5. you .... (an) experience

**Exercise 11

a) *Complete the following sentences.*

1. A closer look .... that things are not what they seem.
2. The author .... her as arrogant and self-assertive.
3. His argument .... weight and .... proof.
4. You .... the conclusion that this is a controversial question.
5. The author .... by saying that 'first things must be dealt with first'.

b) *Find many adjectives/verbs that go together with the keyword.*

1. a(n) .... problem
2. a(n) .... difference
3. The author .... the view that there is still time to act.
4. The author uses .... stylistic devices.
5. You have .... doubt(s) about s.th.
6. You .... an influence.
7. You provide a(n) .... reason to support your idea.

**Exercise 12

Complete the adjective phrase (= adjective + preposition).

1. Are you accustomed ..... staying up late?
2. I'm afraid we are not familiar ..... the rules of the game.
3. You are averse ..... country music, aren't you?
4. Jack is dependent ..... his parents.
5. Are you keen ..... seeing that film?
6. That information is new ..... me.
7. I am concerned ..... our future.
8. The author is concerned ..... the class system in Britain.
9. Are you aware ..... the danger?
10. He is an expert ..... playing squash.

11. My friend is good ..... imitating voices.
12. Our John is intent ..... buying himself a car.
13. Have you always been loyal ..... your teachers?
14. I am absolutely ignorant ..... this fact.
15. I am grateful ..... you. You've done a lot for me.

**Exercise 13

Find adverbs to complete these collocations.

1. *(ausdrücklich)*
   He .... refused to accept any responsibility for it.
2. *(immer mehr)*
   It becomes .... difficult to govern this country.
3. *(völlig)*
   It is .... wrong to believe she will ever change.
4. *(tief)*
   I am .... concerned about your safety.
5. *(nachdrücklich)*
   I .... recommend that hotel; it is not expensive.
6. *(heftig ... äußerst)*
   I must object .... : your proposition is .... unfair.

"Well, Mr Kerslake, I strongly recommend you give up marathon running."

Some Thematic Fields

*Exercise 1

a) *Use the contrast to form sentences with the following:*

conjunction

while, whereas

adverbials

on the one hand ... on the other ...
Yet (am Satzanfang) ...
..., however (zweites Wort im Satz), ...
..., though (am Satzende).

prepositions

in contrast to, in opposition to, unlike

b) *Translate and add these phrases to your active vocabulary:*

s.th. forms a	slight light direct sharp marked striking	contrast with

there is an obvious contrast between ...
s.th. is the very antithesis of s.th.
... is/are very different indeed.
... are very much opposed to each other.

c) *Use the contrast to complete the sentences.*

1. *(im Gegensatz zu)*

'Brave New World' is a so-called welfare tyranny .... '1984', which is based on terror and violence.

2. *(jedoch)*

   In 'Brave New World', ..., drugs play an important part.

3. *(wohingegen)*

   '1984' makes use of threat and intimidation .... / .... 'Brave New World' reduces grown-ups to irresponsible infants.

4. *(auffälliger Kontrast)*

   There is a .... / .... between the educational and other methods that both regimes apply.

5. *(in der Tat sehr unterschiedlich)*

   The two novels are .... / ....

6. *(Anders als)*

   .... the citizens in 'Brave New World' the people of '1984' have to face a drab and miserable existence with few joys and hardly any pleasure.

7. *(das genaue Gegenteil von)*

   One might say that life in 'Brave New World' is .... that in '1984'.

8. *(einerseits ... andererseits)*

   .... Mond's world provides its citizens with all they need and .... they are trained to function as puppets on a string.

* Exercise 2

Our keyword is argument – Translate into German.

a)

to put forward / to advance/to air to agree to to disagree to / to refute / to reject to discuss to consider to give an argument thought	an argument

b)

an argument **can be** ...

sound		weak
effective		questionable
well-founded		irrelevant
cogent	or	shaky
pertinent		unsound
watertight		ill-founded
indisputable		

c)

to argue against / for / in favour of s.th.
to argue with s.b. (!)
the matter is not worth arguing
to weigh the pros and cons
he argued from this that

"You get into an argument, say, about the Gnostic Heresy, or the influence of Palladio on English architecture ..."

***Exercise 3**

Now our keyword is difference *– Translate also.*

a)

Differences between things/situations/people etc. can be ...

great		slight
marked		insignificant
considerable		small
serious	or	subtle
striking		hardly noticeable
essential		
significant		

b)

The difference lies in the fact that ...
Two things/people ... etc. are as different as chalk and cheese.
It makes no difference at all.
It amounts to the same thing.
We have a difference of opinion.
You distinguish / differentiate / discriminate between ....

** Exercise 4

How do you express cause and effect?

conjunction

as
since
in order that
if

adverbs

thus
therefore
so that
consequently
hence
that is why

words/phrases

as a result
in order to + Inf.
owing to
for that (very) reason
as a consequence
that implies
that leads to
so it may be inferred that
one reason is that
one effect is that

Join these pairs of sentences in three different ways.

1. We haven't had much sleep. We are in bad shape today.
2. Have you thought of the upcoming class test? I can't go out tonight.
3. Air travel is becoming a risk these days. You should think twice before flying to America.
4. The Defence Minister was involved in illegal arms sales. He had to resign at once.
5. Our National Health Service is becoming too expensive. Either fees have to be raised or the costs of medical treatment have to be brought down.
6. The greenhouse effect will make itself felt within the next 30–50 years. The western countries will have to change their way of life.

****Exercise 5**

Enlarge your vocabulary of attitudinal adverbs.

1. *(Offensichtlich)*
   .... / .... there are some flaws in the author's line of thought.
2. *(Unglücklicherweise)*
   .... you have failed to mention the central point.
3. *(Überraschenderweise)*
   .... the turning point comes very early in the play.
4. *(Zweifellos)*
   .... / .... it is justified to say that the play is 'well-made'!
5. *(Zwangsläufig)*
   .... teachers 'are right'.
6. *(Seltsamerweise)*
   .... I've seen it all coming. But there was nothing I could do about it.

Sentences

Word Order

Exercise 1

Put the words in the right order.

a)

1. In the story / are / presented / two main characters.
2. This / can / you / see / in ll. 20–25.
3. That problem / solve / they / by talking to each other.
4. For example / writes / the author / that / life / is boring.
5. To prove / this idea / there are / necessary / some facts.
6. The author / discusses / in his text / a problem / of topical interest.
7. I associate / with Christmas / the idea of / snow-covered trees.
8. Christmas / means / for many people / presents and good food.

b)

1. Bob / leads / in the end / the same life / as before.
2. His parents / both / work / and / due to this / think / he / too / should take up / a job / they.
3. In the second unit / is / the life / described / that / Bob / leads / after moving out.
4. The relationship / between / son / and / parents / is / from Bob's side / cool.
5. Bob's parents / see / in him / an idler / not / a son.
6. Is / also / shown / what / the family's living conditions / are / like.

c)

1. In / a mixed ability class / are / all pupils / together.
2. In / one class / are / bright and slow pupils / taught.
3. Also / improved / are / the living conditions.
4. In this text / are / the main clauses / predominant.
5. In the whole text / are / only / facts / given.

Exercise 2

Concentrate on the word order and spot the mistake.

1. The author discusses in his book the pros and cons of living in New York.
2. Everybody associates with New York skyscrapers.
3. That statement can you find on page 3.
4. For example writes the author that New York is the most exciting place in the world.
5. People visit in New York always Manhattan and the Empire State Building.
6. In that book are presented both the good and bad sides of New York.
7. In the text it is said that New Yorkers are proud of their city.

Exercise 3

Keep special attention to the word order again. (Some sentences are correct).

1. In the World State called 'Brave New World' are no deep emotions allowed.
2. That book wrote the author Aldous Huxley in the 1930ies.
3. Soma, a powerful drug that is available to everyone, makes people feel good every minute of their lives.
4. John (= one character in the book) has all the years lived in a different world.
5. There is a moment when John rebels against the way of life that 'Brave New World' citizens are conditioned for.
6. He would everything try to do against the 'Brave New World' state.
7. In rush the soma police with their spray guns.
8. The police pump with their spray guns thick clouds of soma into the air.
9. This world can you only call 'Ugly New World'.

Adverbial Clauses

Exercise 1

Connect each sentence pair in three different ways.

a) as, because, since

b) therefore, that is why, thus, consequently, that is the reason why

1. He had a temperature. He went to see the doctor.
2. We have a holiday tomorrow. We needn't get up early.
3. It had grown dark already. We couldn't go on.
4. You've done a good job today. You won't have to do any homework.
5. His temperature has gone down. The doctor said he might get up the following day.
6. I went home early. The show was a flop.

Exercise 2

Complete these clauses of purpose.

1. My father is bilingual so that ...
2. I took the bus in order to ...
3. Take a taxi to the airport in case ...
4. It was late. He came in silently so as not to ...
5. ... so as to make sure he'd pass the test.
6. ... in order to avoid trouble.
7. ... so he won't forget it this time.
8. ... so that we might enjoy the fine view.

*Exercise 3

Transform the sentences by using in spite of/despite instead of although or vice versa.

1. Although his parents said 'no', he left the house.
2. Despite his excellent interpretation of the poem he claimed he didn't understand it.
3. Although it was difficult, I managed to say 'no'.
4. Although the film was a long one, we did not lose interest.
5. Although he knew that we all depended on his help, he refused to come.
6. In spite of our permanent complaints nothing changed.
7. In spite of her firm belief in ghosts she had never met one.
8. Although my parents said 'yes', I felt uneasy about buying a motorbike.
9. In spite of our contempt for punks in general we like punk rock music.
10. Although we proved him wrong, he would not admit he was wrong.

*Exercise 4

Complete the following clauses of concession.

1. Although he spends a lot on clothes, ...
2. In spite of the fact that she doesn't work hard, ...
3. My friend has never been to the States, although ...
4. Even if he apologizes, ...
5. However hard I tried, ...
6. ..., although the food was good.
7. Despite the fact that I told him to stay, ...

**Exercise 5

Join these sentence pairs by expressing either an antithetic or concessive contrast.

antithetic contrast

but, conversely, by (way of) contrast, instead, by comparison, on the contrary, alternatively,

concessive contrast

however, yet, still, besides, all the same, nevertheless, in spite of that, after all, at the same time

1. I didn't ask her to leave. I tried to make her stay for another hour.
2. He has been here for two weeks only. He has achieved more than we expected.
3. The hotel caught fire. No hotel guest was killed.
4. Don't be too aggressive. You shouldn't be too timid.
5. He doesn't listen. He just sits and day-dreams.
6. She hadn't slept for days. She looked as fresh as a daisy.
7. So far the weather has been bad indeed. We are enjoying our stay.

Relative Clauses

Exercise 1

Join the sentence pairs. Leave out the relative pronoun where possible.

1. Is that the new Mercedes model? You pointed it out to me the other day.
2. This is the police officer. I asked him about the way this morning.
3. The policemen found it difficult to keep calm. They were all very young.
4. Last year I revisited the place. I used to live in that place for 20 years.
5. Bring me the magazine. I left it on the table. The table stands near the window.
6. The problem has been settled. You were arguing about it last night. It was not an easy job I tell you.

*Exercise 2

Translate these relative clauses.

1. Alles, was er besaß, wurde gestohlen.
2. Das passierte erst am Tag zuvor, was ihn sehr ärgerlich gemacht hat.
3. Sein Vater, der oben im Haus wohnte, war schon eingeschlafen gewesen.
4. Die Dinge, die er am meisten benötigte, waren sein Reisepaß und sein Führerschein.
5. Der Vater erzählte, was er mitbekommen hatte: nichts, was den Sohn keinesfalls überraschte.
6. Was immer die Polizei ihm klarzumachen versuchte, er wußte, daß er das, was wertvoll war, nicht wiedersehen würde.

*Exercise 3

Spot the mistake. Keep special attention to relative clauses.

a)

1. He is definitely the man exploits his employees without scruples.
2. The executive addresses his employees who he does not remember their names.
3. The bowler hat serves as a symbol of men which are successful.
4. A modern businessman has no scruple to fire his employees he has known for years.
5. That rudeness reminds me of the early capitalist attitude which principle was 'Eat or be Eaten'.
6. All what counts for him is salesfigures and profit.
7. An employee longs to be respected and treated as a human being, whereby his age does not matter.
8. He has tried to obtain a job who is beyond his reach.

b)

1. Willy kindly addresses Howard Wagner, who he finds sitting behind his voluminous desk.
2. He appears to be the man exploits his employees without the slightest scruples.

3. The businessman Howard does not hesitate to fire his employee he has known for years.
4. This business policy reminds of Darwinism which main principle is 'survival of the fittest.'
5. All what counts for Howard is sales figures.
6. A successful businessman has the right to be respected, even loved, whereby it does not matter how old he is.

Style

***Exercise 1**

The reference must be clear. Transform the sentences.

1. Shouting across the room, nobody understood what I wanted to say.
2. I ran into her, crossing the room.
3. Dressed in the latest fashion, I had the impression they were all models.
4. Blowing their horns, the main roads were congested with cars.
5. I regret insulting you deeply.
6. When finally arrived, we welcomed our friends.
7. We locked every door and window afraid of burglars.
8. Though asking more than once for the way, nobody could tell us where to go.

***Exercise 2**

Spot the mistake. The reference is incorrect or unclear.

1. The president tells the CBS correspondent that he will announce the tax plan soon.
2. The president's tax cuts make sense because they think that is necessary for our country.
3. He stated that everyone no matter how much they earned would have to pay more taxes.
4. His aide's advice: if the higher taxes bother the taxpayers, cut them.
5. At one time the president was a model student at Harvard which many people still remember.
6. Having studied the speech must be regarded as poor rhetoric.
7. When the president tried to ring up his campaign manager, he dialled the wrong number.

**Exercise 3

These sentences sound confusing: Rewrite them.

1. When reading this text for the first time, it seems rather difficult to understand.
2. I have seen accidents happen so often that I am so used to seeing them that I simply overlook them now.
3. The climax of the story comes in the two concluding lines. Nevertheless one can find other climaxes, too, but these are not so striking.
4. The atmosphere in the first part is dark and gloomy and one can compare it to the classroom in the other story we read.
5. In contrast to the first ten lines which are marked by a general approach to the topic the author then goes into detail.
6. The example means, that, since nobody is perfect, he should be forgiven that he behaved in the wrong way, which is what the author wants to point out.

*Exercise 4

Use the following to emphasize or tone down the statements given:

emphasizers

certainly	frankly
definitely	absolutely
... indeed	completely
obviously	entirely
honestly	badly
simply	

downtoners

rather	scarcely
more or less	not ... at all
partly	to some extent
somewhat	not ... in the least
a bit	
barely	

1. I don't know what he wants.
2. That event influenced his actions in later life.
3. That's wrong; I, for my part, should say that.
4. I forgot about her birthday.
5. I enjoyed the show; it was well organized.
6. I enjoyed the show; most of it was boring.
7. In the grammar test he failed; no correct answer.

8. In the grammar test he failed; half his answers are o.k.
9. I agree to your statement; it convinces me.
10. I agree to your statement; I would perhaps add another idea.
11. I can't follow you there; that's rubbish!
12. I can follow you there; that's rubbish!

***Exercise 5**

Enlarge your vocabulary by translating into German. Keep special attention to sentence openings.

1. It is well-known that ...
2. It is rather unlikely that ...
3. I suppose it is justified to say that ...
4. For reasons already stated ...
5. To put it at its simplest ...
6. The question arises if ...
7. Let's assume that ...
8. Needless to say that ...
9. It stands to reason that ...
10. Judging by ...
11. If I remember rightly ...
12. When it comes to ...
13. No matter how/when/where/what ...
14. In the long run ...
15. The fact remains that ...
16. It is safe to say that ...
17. It is in the nature of things that ...
18. Curiously enough ...

***Exercise 6**

Translate and find at least two versions for the underlined word.

1. <u>Außerdem</u> möchte ich erwähnen, daß das ganz unmöglich ist.
2. Er kam nicht; <u>infolgedessen</u> fehlte uns eine männliche Person.
3. Hör auf zu reden; <u>statt dessen</u> solltest du lieber zuhören lernen.
4. <u>Übrigens</u>, hast du schon den Film von Stanley Kubrik gesehen?
5. Der Film zielt gegen den Krieg, <u>d.h.</u> er ist ein Antikriegsfilm.
6. Die Mannschaft konnte nicht mehr gewinnen; <u>nichtsdestoweniger</u> kämpfte sie bis zum Ende.

*Exercise 7

Use the following correlatives to join the sentence pairs.

not only ... but also ...
both ... and ...
either ... or ...
neither ... nor ...
not ... either.

The ... the ...

as early / late / far as ...

1. He is (not) bright. He is (not) hard-working.
2. He sold his car. He sold his bike.
3. We shall go by train this year. We shall go by plane this year.
4. That is .... a solution ....
5. The monastery was built .... 950 A.D.
6. Our daughter came home .... 3 o'clock this morning.
7. We will travel .... Munich today.
8. You won't be there? I will .... come ....
9. .... harder you work .... better your pay will be.
10. The taxi driver was (not) killed in the accident. The passenger was (not) killed in the accident.

**Exercise 8

Two characteristics of English style are forcefulness and fluency.

forcefulness

prefer verb constructions to nominal style
use personal grammatical subjects not abstractions
use verbs in active

Rewrite the following sentences.

1. The author's use of metaphors is striking.
2. It was proved to us that we were wrong.
3. The poet gives a portrait of the city of Chicago.

4. By means of adjectives the impression of gloom is evoked.
5. I am of the opinion that the author's view is one-sided.
6. The re-establishment of contact to the audience occurs in l. 67.
7. In the main part the topic of '...' is enlarged on by the author.
8. The author gives a representation of the punk movement.

Forcefulness ...

fluency

form comparatively short sentences, split "clumsy sentences" into 2 or 3 smaller units
in general place subclauses before the main clause
include only related ideas in one sentence

Rewrite the following sentences.

1. He was a fairly popular teacher, working hard to please his students.
2. Although he started early, he did not make it in time on account of the traffic jam in spite of the extra tip he promised the taxi driver.
3. She decided not to get married although she was a popular girl and although she was proposed to quite often – at least for the time being.
4. We were able to afford the new car having earned an extra premium.
5. E. Pound uses a rich metaphorical language, a fact which deserves to be mentioned since metaphors are a typical poetic device the originality of which decides about the quality of the poem, i.e. whether a text can be considered as interesting or as boring.

**Exercise 9

Two further characteristics of clear English are concreteness and precision.

concreteness

do not use vague or (too many) abstract nouns/adjectives
try to find exact words

Rewrite these sentences.

1. The character of ... has some positive aspects.
2. He behaves kind of friendly towards strangers.
3. Comparing 'A' and 'B' there are quite a few differences that should be mentioned.
4. Their relationship is not a good one.
5. The author describes the main character in a very negative way.

precision

exclude all unnecessary words
try to write consistent syntax
stick to the tense you have chosen

Rewrite these sentences.

1. He begins by describing the setting, and, in the following, he went on to introduce his characters.
2. The final conclusion can be found in ll. 47–51.
3. Throughout the whole text the author remains on an abstract level.
4. The impression you get is something like a discussion between author and reader.
5. These ideas just mentioned make me think of the 1950ies.
6. The author's central problem can be expressed as the question of when to start doing something about the environmental crisis.
7. According to his opinion it is five past twelve.

**Exercise 10

Balanced sentences are very common in English.

balanced sentences

coordinated words/phrases take the same grammatical form
parallel structures must be grammatically parallel

Rewrite these sentences.

1. The image in l. 12 not only suggests his helplessness but also his laziness.
2. The topics the author deals with are swimming, surfing, and to lie on the beach.
3. What he said and the things he meant were not the same.
4. He both praised the food and the accomodation in the small hotel.
5. By examining the author's choice of words and by the study of his syntax you can establish the text form.
6. The author explains the present situation and that he is convinced of an immediate change.

**Exercise 11

How to achieve emphasis in your writing:

end-focus

try to answer in the passive

Rewrite these sentences.

1. Who won World War II? (The Allied Forces)
2. What is the cause of cancer? (Among other things it is smoking)
3. Was Columbus the first to discover America? (Norsemen; in the 10th or 11th century)

contrastive focus

add a suitable negative element

Rewrite these sentences.

1. I think I'll have red wine, not .... , today.
2. It was in the south of Germany, not .... , where I lived for 20 years.
3. This is a problem that a computer, rather than .... , could solve easily.
4. You won't make it by .... but by working hard.

cleavage

cleft sentences with introductory 'it'

Change these sentences accordingly.

1. I want to watch the sports channel. It is ....
2. The class test took a long time to write because it raised many difficult questions.
3. The party got going after the Joneses had left.
4. The class speaker reported this incident to the head master. (3 versions!)

**Exercise 12

a) *It is considered poor style to write as in the following sentences. Find better solutions.*

1. We get to know that he is a pilot.
2. He tries to get into contact with us.
3. The reader gets more and more involved.
4. This gets clearer as we read on.

b) *Avoid long verb phrases.*

1. The author gives a presentation of class war in the U.K.
2. She is of the opinion that we must act now.
3. He tries to give a justification of chemical warfare.
4. In his articles he gives a portrait of Britain in the nineties.

**Exercise 13

Improve your style of writing. Avoid unnecessary shift in tense / point of view / active / passive, etc.
Rewrite these sentences.

1. In the first part he introduces his thesis ... in the last part he confirmed it again.
2. The author strives to write simple and straight forward sentences but abstract terms are used from time to time, too.
3. He points out that we have gone too far and that one must think of our grandchildren.
4. Each of us will be asked about our flight tickets.
5. If we have success and won the match, we will make the playoffs.
6. The one point I do not understand are the fees charged at this school.

Revision Test 1

Part 1

Make sure of your vocabulary.

1. *(wird sichtbar)*
   This aspect .... in ll. 17–20.
2. *(auch keine)*
   That is .... solution ....
3. *(inkonsequent)*
   The way he argues is ....
4. *(schlußfolgern)*
   So we can .... that it is high time to do s.th..
5. *(behauptet)*
   The author .... that without providing evidence.
6. *(Es ist wichtig, zu unterscheiden zwischen)*
   .... cause and effect.
7. *(will, daß)*
   I want .... you .... get along with each other.
8. *(soll)*
   The newspaper comment .... stir up public opinion.
9. *(wesentlich)*
   Going abroad while you are young is a .... experience.
10. *(Zwar ...)*
    .... football is a marvellous game but look at the fans!

Part 2

Pick the right preposition (/––/= keine Präposition setzen).

1. New games like 'Money Management Mania' and 'Investment Seminars for Kids' are good examples *(of/for/in)* ..... America's becoming competitive again, writes Newsweek.
2. Mini-yuppies and 15-year-old capitalists seem to be more and more characteristic *(for/about/of)* ..... U.S. teenagers in the 1980ies.

3. *(In/For/To)* ..... my mind that is a questionable tendency to be observed now.
4. You might discuss *(about/––/over)* ..... that question in class.
5. By the way, what is your attitude *(towards/to/of)* ..... money?
6. Can you explain *(––/about/to)* ..... me who is responsible for that kind of thing?
7. I simply object *(with/to/––)* ..... teaching kids how to multiply their money like smart tycoons.
8. Grown-ups should reflect *(––/about/on)* ..... what is best for the young.
9. Rather than be encouraged kids should be warned *(before/against/of)* ..... 'dreaming the big money dream' (Newsweek).
10. This is no discrimination *(of/about/against)* ..... part-time jobbers or a little money-making on the side, though.

Part 3

Translate into English. Beware of "false friends".

1. Siehst du oft 'Seifenopern' im Fernsehen?
2. Sieh dorthin! Was kannst du sehen?
3. Ich versuchte, wegzusehen, aber ich konnte nicht anders, als den Unfall anzusehen.
4. Für diesen Bericht benötigen wir viele Informationen.
5. Laß mich dir einige Ratschläge geben.

Part 4

Spot the one spelling mistake in each sentence.

1. Do you want to loose the match? Come on!
2. A relativ clause can be 'that'-marked.
3. I would like to belive what you are telling me. Unfortunately I can't.

4. The text can be devided into five major sections.
5. He is a human beeing after all.
6. They want to find out about it themselfs.
7. Do you practice judo every day?
8. That is none of your busyness.
9. The prove of that can be found in ll. 21–22.
10. Can you give me a satisfactory explaination for your conduct?

Part 5

Complete these collocations.

1. Finally the author drew the .... by saying: not with me!
2. After weighing the .... and .... he made up his mind.
3. Our Government does everything to .... the gap between the rich and the poor.
4. It is a privilege to be .... in(to) a favourable home environment.
5. Taking everything into .... one can say the author gives a true picture of the situation.
6. Intelligent as she is, she always has an opinion ....
7. Can you provide .... from the text for your interesting idea?
8. The argument he .... is very much to the point.
9. What is .... he speaks quite movingly.
10. It is no wonder that he .... his goal in the end.

Part 6

Translate into English. Beware of the tenses.

1. Unser Engländer lebt seit 10 Jahren bei uns in Deutschland.
2. Letztes Jahr hat er seine Ferien „auf der Insel" verbracht.
3. Er ist auch schon oft in Spanien gewesen.
4. Wenn du ihn fragen würdest, würde er sagen, sein Lieblingsland sei Spanien.

5. Er ist schon oft gefragt worden, wie ihm Deutschland gefällt.
6. Wenn er Deutscher wäre, würde er nirgendwo anders leben wollen.
7. Er versucht schon seit Jahren, einen gut bezahlten Job in Spanien zu bekommen.
8. Er hätte längst einen Job dort, wenn er Spanisch gelernt hätte.
9. Letzten Monat ist er wieder nach Spanien gefahren.
10. Wenn er sehr viel Glück hat, kann er vielleicht nächstes Jahr in Spanien arbeiten.

Part 7

Rewrite these sentences. Keep special attention to the word order.

1. He solves in his mind easily the problem of hunger in the world.
2. That also is my idea about it.
3. In the northern hemisphere are the wealthy nations to be found.
4. The hunger problem can you only solve on a worldwide scale.
5. All over the world exist nations who to eat have enough.

Part 8

Find a synonym for the underlined word.

1. In the next few decades a new problem will develop: our water supplies.
2. That is an essential point to be kept in mind.
3. The author contrasts the Western democracies and the developing countries.
4. He underscores the necessity of international solidarity.
5. In the main part of the article he accumulates striking examples to support his thesis.
6. Our present lethargy will lead to an international crisis.
7. In the Third World you are faced with hardship and misery.
8. What is the attitude you assume towards the financial problems of the developing countries?
9. What are the experiences you have gathered on your trip to the U.S.?
10. From my point of view that is sheer nonsense!

Part 9

Watch your grammar. Translate German 'was'.

1. Das ist es, was ich wissen wollte.
2. Ihr Kommen war, was niemand erwartet hatte, die Sensation.
3. Das ganze Geld war weg, was niemanden überraschte.
4. Er tat, was er konnte, um uns zu helfen.
5. Sie hat einen Grund für ihr Fehlen, was alles in einem anderen Licht erscheinen läßt.

Points total: 75

Points scored:

Revision Test 2

Part 1

Check the construction of each verb and spot the mistake.

1. The author explained us what he thought.
2. We thought to be able to arrive in time.
3. He was looking forward to meet new people.
4. The teacher made him answering in a full sentence.
5. He had to get used to eat with a knife and a fork.

Part 2

Translate these collocations into English.

1. um es kurz zu machen ...
2. alles in allem ...
3. ein stichhaltiges Argument
4. ein Argument zurückweisen
5. zweifellos ...
6. die Frage erhebt sich, ob ...
7. wenn man nach ... urteilt ...
8. er neigt zu der Auffassung, daß ...
9. sich etwas lebhaft vorstellen
10. etwas für selbstverständlich halten

Part 3

the or **'zero'-article**

1. Are you afraid of ..... death?
2. ..... life is shorter than you think and ..... death may be around the corner.
3. I did not have ..... time I needed for watching ..... TV programmes I was interested in.
4. What do you think of ..... presentation of ..... reality on ..... TV?
5. ..... local TV stations did not broadcast ..... truth of the violent conflict.

Part 4

Find a suitable antonym (= word/expression opposed in meaning).

1. There's a significant difference between the two texts.
2. The atmosphere in this group is strained.
3. The author attacks the idea that …
4. In those days things used to be different.
5. She admits having taken the money.
6. I'm quite certain that there's something fishy about it.
7. That's definitely impossible.
8. Your argument seems well-founded.
9. The demonstrators expressed their feelings openly.

Part 5

Translate these sentences.

a)

1. Das ist ein klares Zeichen für deine Intoleranz.
2. Schlangestehen ist typisch für die Briten.

b)

1. Sag mir, wie Windsurfen wirklich ist.
2. Die Geschichte war stinklangweilig, wie?
3. Wie ich es sehe, gibt es keinen Ausweg.

Part 6

Translate but beware of "false friends".

1. Er ist mit seiner Arbeit fertig.
2. Eine schlechte Nachricht ist eine gute Nachricht.
3. Das ist eine Frage von aktuellem Interesse.
4. Er hat nahezu keine Chance.
5. Wir haben zumindest unser Bestes gegeben.

Part 7

Make sure of your vocabulary.

1. *(im Gegensatz zu)*
   South Africa is a dangerous place these days .... Scandinavia which is a calm area.
2. *(bringt)*
   In l. 33 the author .... a striking argument.
3. *(paradox)*
   It is .... when a minority dominates a majority.
4. *(behauptet)*
   The author .... that young people shirk responsibility.
5. *(verdient)*
   Your enormous effort .... recognition.
6. *(dienen)*
   This may .... a good example of British fairplay.
7. *(heutige)*
   The .... situation on the job market is discouraging.
8. *(Punkt der Kritik)*
   The most important .... is that your view is prejudiced.
9. *(ist sinnvoll)*
   That interpretation ...., doesn't it? / isn't it?
10. *(kommt auf dasselbe heraus)*
    Whether we stay or leave ....

Part 8

Translate. Keep special attention to the forms of the future.

1. Hast du vor, nächste Woche zu kommen?
2. Er wird morgen früh um 6:15 fahren.
3. Nächsten Monat werden wir in Spanien in der Sonne liegen.
4. Es wird mit großer Wahrscheinlichkeit gleich regnen.
5. Es wird morgen überall sonnig sein.

Part 9

Complete these collocations.

1. My sisters are as different as ....
2. I was .... impressed by the pope's speech.
3. The author disapproves of .... that social injustice can't be helped.
4. The long and .... I have forgotten my car keys.
5. For .... already stated there is no alternative.
6. It stands to .... that the author is wrong.
7. That is easier said than ....
8. If you .... me, simply forget about it!
9. After weighing the .... and .... we must make up our minds now.
10. I am quite .... that this is the way we should vote.

Part 10

Check the vocabulary. Spot the mistake.

1. Have you ever thought of the follows of your behaviour?
2. Why don't we prove the new teacher's sense of humour today?
3. Don't let the doors open when you go.
4. Are you going to except his offer or not?
5. You're right, that's a very senseful question.

Points total: 70

Points scored:

Revision Test 3

Part 1

Spelling

1. the author's ch...ce of words
2. I am refe...ing to ll. 15–17.
3. It was a great d...sillusion.
4. He d...scribes the landscape.
5. Have you any pro... *(Beweis)*?

Part 2

Translate but beware of "false friends".

1. Wessen Buch hast du da?
2. das Problem und seine Lösung
3. Kannst du eventuell morgen kommen?
4. Er ist sehr selbstbewußt.
5. Sie ist eine sympathische Person.
6. Das ist auch nicht korrekt.
7. Machst du deine Hausaufgaben?
8. Der Autor bleibt sehr abstrakt.
9. Er hat sich für Greenpeace engagiert.

Part 3

Do you know your prepositions? Keep special attention to a) German 'bei' and b) German 'durch'.

a)

1. Do you still live *(by/with/for)* ..... your parents?
2. I spent my holidays *(in/by/near)* ..... St. Ives in Cornwall.
3. I've got a part-time job *(with/by/at)* ..... McDonald's.

b)

1. *(By/because of/by means of)* ..... the weather we were late.
2. The man was arrested *(through/by/owing to)* ..... the police.
3. The author tries to convince the reader *(by/with/by means of)* ..... well-known examples.

c)

1. *(Im Hinblick auf)*
   .... the fact that the decision has been taken let's forget about it.
2. *(gemäß)*
   He did not behave .... the rules.
3. *(im Verhältnis zu)*
   The sentence was too severe .... the offence he committed.
4. *(dank)*
   She was easy to work with .... her professional attitude.

Part 4

adjective or **adverb**

1. *(indirekt)*
   The author characterizes his figures ....
2. *(Implizit)*
   .... the author is trying to say that we are in danger.
3. *(indirekt)*
   Speech is a means of .... characterization.
4. *(gut)*
   Is your job .... paid?
5. *(anschaulich)*
   The poet describes the scene ....

Part 5

Find a suitable synonym for the underlined word(s).

1. 'Parallelism' is a frequently used stylistic means.
2. The author uses unusual symbols in his poem.

3. He <u>realizes</u> his own weaknesses.
4. That is one of the most <u>pressing</u> problems I know of.
5. We can sense the <u>tensed-up</u> atmosphere in the room.
6. An example of his strangeness <u>can be found</u> in ll. 1–5.
7. The author <u>conveys</u> to us what he personally thinks of it.
8. The long illness <u>has influenced</u> his state of mind.
9. The coach said we all must <u>be held responsible for</u> this last defeat.
10. Throughout the text he <u>remains on an abstract level</u>.

Part 6

Check the vocabulary. Spot the mistake and correct it.

1. His critic of the new film was devastating.
2. The author brings a lot of convincing examples.
3. As she is very sensible, my friend is often upset about things.
4. A 'law-and-order' policy has its good.
5. Why don't you let her alone for a while?
6. The chairman asked the committee to except his proposition.
7. We were all very exciting when the guest of honour was led in.
8. We simply have to adopt to our environment.
9. The text shall impress the readers and make them take actions.

Part 7

Complete these <u>collocations</u>.

1. It is in .... of things that man is mortal.
2. The author .... a rather sarcastic attitude towards feminism.
3. It is/seems .... to say that Germany's motorcars are among the best.
4. In the following the author goes into ....
5. I must say that his arguments carry ....
6. My own experience .... that we have no time lose.

7. That is a(n) (+) .... / a(n) (–) .... argument.

8. In l. 20 we can observe a(n) (+) .... / a(n) (–) .... contrast.

Part 8

How about your vocabulary of text analysis? Translate into English.

1. Man kann unterscheiden zwischen ...
2. Man kann behaupten, daß ...
3. Diese Szene bildet den Höhepunkt.
4. Seine (innere) Spannung steigt.
5. Der Autor macht konkrete Angaben zu ...
6. Ehrlich gesagt ist das Blödsinn!
7. Der Autor spielt auf bekannte Personen an.
8. Er nimmt an, daß ...
9. Was mich etwas verwirrt, ist, daß ...
10. Der Autor legt nahe, daß ...

Part 9

Supply a suitable verb.

1. His main thesis *(lautet)* .... as follows.
2. The author's imagery *(ruft hervor)* .... feelings of uneasiness.
3. She *(soll)* .... to be awarded the Nobel Prize this year.
4. He struggled hard *(erreichen)* to .... a better position in life.
5. In his text the writer *(stellt gegenüber)* .... two very different views.

Points total: 73

Points scored:

Revision Test 4

Part 1

Spelling

1. Let's talk about TV and i... effect on heavy viewers.
2. I do not bel...ve TV is a good thing.
3. Kids who... parents are divorced.
4. There is a respons...bility for parents after all.
5. Does that make sen...e to you?

Part 2

Translate but beware of "false friends".

1. Das nenne ich unmenschlich.
2. Sie ist sehr selbstbewußt.
3. Er muß mit der Situation klarkommen.
4. Es ist zu sagen, daß beide recht haben.
5. Wir brauchen weitere Informationen.
6. Der Text soll komisch sein?
7. Er argumentiert sehr einseitig.
8. Eine sinnvolle Antwort!
9. Er wird eventuell kommen.
10. Ein sympathischer Kerl!

Part 3

Find a synonym for the underlined word(s).

1. Your idea throws new light on our text.
2. He refuses to take full responsibility.
3. Obviously there is no other choice.
4. I'm almost certain that this is so.
5. This contributes to the effect intended.
6. The setting evokes an atmosphere of mystery.
7. His thoughts revolve around making money.
8. She realized that she was alone in the room.
9. He gives a close analysis of the text.
10. The author keeps to facts. He does not comment on them.

Part 4

Do you know your prepositions?

1. Are you familiar ..... British pub food?
2. I am very much concerned ..... my parent's health.
3. Are you keen ..... dating English-speaking boys?
4. This is quite new ..... us.
5. As a psychologist she is accustomed ..... listening patiently.

Part 5

How about your vocabulary of text analysis? Translate into English.

1. Das ist eine Behauptung. Wo ist dein Beweis?
2. Er kommt zu dem Schluß, daß ...
3. Ihr Stil ist nüchtern und sachlich.
4. Seine Beispiele sind anschaulich.
5. Der Autor trifft eine Unterscheidung zwischen ...
6. Er enthält sich eines persönlichen Kommentars.

7. Das ist genau der Grund, weshalb ...
8. 'A' liegt im Widerstreit mit sich selbst.
9. Der Konflikt bleibt ungelöst.
10. Sie widerlegt das Argument, daß ...

Part 6

Complete these collocations.

a) verb + (intensifying) adverb
adjective + (intensifying) adverb

1. The Prime Minister .... refused to take action.
2. She believed the opposition was .... wrong.
3. She .... objected to even consider the proposition.
4. Mrs Thatcher said she was .... concerned about Britain's future.
5. Governing the country was becoming .... difficult she added.

b) *Find a suitable verb.*

1. A closer look .... that things are not that easy.
2. He .... the reader's attention to the fact that driving at any speed is unsafe.
3. The author .... the reader's interest by being mysterious.
4. The author .... the thesis that the solution is just around the corner.
5. He .... the view that we just have to look for it.

Part 7

Check the vocabulary and spot the mistake.

1. What are the criterias of a good summary?
2. The second unit contains ll. 30–35.
3. She makes the experience that most Germans are very unfriendly.
4. This is a chance for you to show what you can.

5. The text remembers me of a film I've seen on TV.
6. The author's arguments manage that the reader begins to change his mind.
7. As far as I am concerned I would say that is too dangerous.
8. In opposite to me you have already been to America.
9. Suddenly he remarked a man following him.
10. The author employs familiar language.

Part 8

adjective or **adverb**

1. I'm sure our dreams will come tru..... one day.
2. This is real..... crazy.
3. My friend says I'm a real..... madman.
4. She is deep..... in love with Bob.
5. My remark was meant ironical.....

Points total: 65

Points scored:

Die „zehn Todsünden" des Grundkursschülers

Exercise 1

a) *Keep special attention to the verb forms and the "third-person-sing.-s".*

s or **not**

1. Er will nicht aufgeben.
2. Er braucht nicht zu warten.
3. Er darf nicht versagen.
4. Sie glaubt mir nicht.
5. Sie plant, nach England zu gehen.
6. Sie fragt ihn, ob er Zeit habe.

b) **been** or **be**

1. Ich bin krank gewesen.
2. Morgen um 8 Uhr werden wir wahrscheinlich Tennis spielen.
3. Das wäre sonst *(otherwise)* klar gewesen.
4. Er sagte, er hätte es gewußt, wenn er ruhiger gewesen wäre.
5. Man (!) darf ihn nicht vergessen; ihm ist erzählt worden, daß wir da sein werden.
6. Es heißt, ich sei zum Sprecher gemacht worden; das muß überprüft werden. Ich wäre sonst sehr enttäuscht.

c) *Check the verbs and spot the mistakes.*

1. He was been out of the house for years.
2. He wants not to be treated as a coward.
3. He is hatred by his students.
4. If they have success and reached the place in time, that might be advantageous.

5. I have tried to make him clear what our world is like.
6. She answeres that she has no one to talk to.
7. She said me that everything was all right.
8. Are you looking forward to spend your holidays in Greece this year?
9. We all thought to be safe now that we were on land again.
10. In the main part the author explains us what he has mind.
11. The captain wanted that the passengers fastened their seat belts.
12. Nobody is interesting in her feelings. She feels lost.
13. There are enough good things to be enjoyed to make life worth to live.

Exercise 2

Complete the pattern and translate into English. Make sure your construction of the conditional clauses is correct.

subclause: If ...	main clause
present	
	conditional I, II
past perfect	

1. Der Leistungssport *(competitive sport)* wäre nicht so gefährlich, wenn Sportärzte verantwortungsvoller handeln würden.
2. Wenn Kinder schon mit drei Jahren ernsthaft trainieren, hören *(quit)* sie oft mit 13 oder 14 Jahren auf. Sie haben genug.
3. Manch ein Jugendlicher hätte seine Freude am Sport nicht verloren, wenn er/sie nicht so hart hätten trainieren müssen.
4. Andererseits – wenn man nicht früh beginnt, wird man sich nie für nationale oder internationale Meisterschaften qualifizieren.
5. Viele Sportstars wären nicht so bekannt geworden, wenn sie nicht so viele sportliche Siege errungen hätten.
6. Eltern wären besser beraten *(to be better advised),* wenn sie ihre Kinder nicht für sportliche Miniaturerwachsene *(pocket adults)* halten würden.

Exercise 3

Translate the following sentences.

klar – **unklar**

1. Es ist völlig klar, daß ihr den Text bis morgen lesen müßt.
2. Der Sinn des Textes bleibt mir ziemlich unklar.
3. Du mußt dir darüber klarwerden, daß das unmöglich ist.
4. Er hat keine Wahl; er muß mit der Situation klarkommen.
5. Ich habe nur eine sehr unklare Vorstellung von dem Problem.
6. Mir ist nicht ganz klar, was du meinst.
7. Der Autor macht uns das anhand von Beispielen klar.
8. Haben wir alle Unklarheiten beseitigt?
9. Das ist meines Erachtens ein klarer Beweis.

Exercise 4

Do you know your prepositions?

a)

1. Out-of-town shopping centres are typical ..... Britain in the 90ies.
2. In an article ..... Jean Carr you can get more information ..... the new shopping centres.
3. The author does not warn us ..... that development; she simply gives examples ..... the new trend.
4. She divides the trend ..... 'megacentres' and 'retail parks', both of which she explains ..... the reader at length.
5. If you go ..... Metro Centre near Gateshead/Tyneside for example, you will be tempted to stay ..... the centre all day long.
6. Huge areas of retailing, a miniature Disneyland, a Space City (video games) hotels and restaurants are characteristic ..... such a centre.

7. ..... my mind those megacentres are designed to influence consumer attitudes.
8. The centres are vital ..... developers and owners only.
9. Reflect ..... that and discuss ..... it in class if you feel like it.

b)

1. The text consists ..... five units.
2. The second paragraph is rich ..... adverbial clauses.
3. It also contains ..... quite a few relative clauses.
4. In the main part the author refers ..... the latest statistics.
5. This idea can be proved ..... our text, cf. ll. 11–13.
6. The article ..... 'streaming' in British schools is quite interesting.
7. You stream students ..... *(gemäß)* their abilities.
8. The author's style is marked ..... well-balanced sentence structures.
9. Are you aware of the striking contrast ..... scene 1 ..... scene 2?
10. ..... his point of view the question is rather complicated.

Exercise 5

adjective or **adverb**

1. That is a tru..... deep conflict.
2. His dream has come tru...... .
3. The play's real..... conflict occurs in Act I.
4. What you are saying is real..... tru...... .
5. Is this real..... or imaginary?
6. Is that real..... so?
7. My dad is a real..... madman.
8. Yours tru..... , James.
9. She is doing real..... well at school.

10. This is real..... very difficult.
11. His tru..... love is Brenda.
12. He is tru..... in love with Brenda.

Exercise 6

Put the words in the right order.

1. This text/is/in the third person/written.
2. Here/is/substitutionary narration/in action.
3. He/assumes/also/the attitude of/an observer.
4. He/has to travel/day in day out/the same route.
5. Life/is/for him/depressing and dispiriting.

Exercise 7

Find the correct relative pronouns.

1. In ‘1984’ Orwell describes a regime .... motto is ‘love is hate’.
2. We witness a situation .... the Party assumes complete control over every citizen.
3. There is a society .... aims differ greatly from those of the ‘Brave New World’.
4. How do you feel about a world like the one .... O’Brien has it in mind?
5. There are always some .... are opposed to totalitarian regimes.
6. Those are people .... I think in terms of ‘heroes’.
7. For a regime based on suspicion and hatred there is always an enemy .... has to be defeated.
8. We watched a lot of film scenes from ‘1984’, some .... were quite moving.

Exercise 8

ing-form or **infinitive**

1. My friend is not used to .... *(read)* many books.
2. She believes .... *(be)* back by ten tonight.
3. There is no doubt that she is capable of .... *(fulfil)* the task.
4. ‘Dynasty’ has made .... *(Joan Collins; a star)*.
5. The teacher made us .... *(stay)* for another hour.
6. We’ve been looking forward to .... *(meet)* him for some time.

Exercise 9

Do not trust some of your best friends.

1. *(bringt)*
   To support his thesis the author .... some examples.
2. *(will, daß wir)*
   The author .... think about his view.
3. *(soll)*
   The text .... illustrate the risks of scientific research.
4. *(Mit ... ist gemeint, daß)*
   The use of the word ‘solidarity’ .... that people should cooperate instead of fighting against each other.
5. *(Bei ...)*
   .... G. Orwell this is very different.
6. *(auch nicht)*
   I can’t approve of that ....
7. *(was)*
   She works as a shop-assistant, ... must be dull and tedious.
8. *(sagst)*
   She .... her parents that she will move out.
9. *(läßt)*
   This .... him feel sure that he is right.

10. *(einen eigenen)*
At 18 he already had .... car ....

11. *(meint)*
The author .... that the Brits should withdraw from Northern Ireland.

12. *(ihm klarmachen)*
The father tries to .... that he cannot stay with them.

Exercise 10

Vocabulary of text analysis: translate.

Der Autor
- vertritt die These, daß ...
- nimmt an, daß ...
- widerspricht, indem er ...
- widerlegt das Argument, daß ...
- liefert Beweise für ...
- führt Beispiele an für ...
- zitiert eine anerkannte Persönlichkeit ...
- bezieht sich auf anerkannte Tatsachen ...
- schlußfolgert, daß ...
- kommt zu dem Schluß, daß ...

Ulrich Klinge

Training
Success in English

Grammar, Vocabulary, Spelling

Sekundarstufe II

Lösungsheft

Ernst Klett Verlag
Stuttgart Düsseldorf Leipzig

Satz: G. Müller, Heilbronn
Druck: Wilhelm Röck, Weinsberg
Beilage zu 3-12-922112-3

Überprüfen Sie Ihr Wissen

Part 1

1. ---
2. a
3. a
4. ---
5. an

Part 2

1. opinion
2. meaning
3. reminds me
4. remember
5. interested

Part 3

1. What would you do if someone gave you $ 1,000?
2. If I were young again, I would do many things in a different way.
3. He would have come if we had invited him.
4. If you had told us everything, we would not have been so surprised.
5. I would not claim that if I did not know that.

Part 4

1. typical of
2. depends on
3. regarded as/considered as
4. among other things
5. includes/gives
6. hence (it) follows
7. refers to
8. divides/breaks into
9. comprises
10. becomes evident/apparent

Part 5

1. by
2. with ... by ... from
3. with ... in
4. after ... by
5. ---/from (in)
6. with

Part 6

1. always
2. than
3. describe
4. families
5. accept
6. another
7. responsibility
8. life
9. sense
10. character

Part 7

1. She looked at him kindly/in a friendly way.
2. That is becoming clear to me.
3. That is clearly a problem we must talk about.

4. He describes the man in detail.
5. The author addresses the reader directly.

Part 8

1. At last/Eventually
2. view
3. achieved
4. give evidence of/endorse
5. make us understand
6. falls into
7. covers
8. is supposed to/is intended to
9. To my mind
10. As a first step

Part 9

a) 1. Wenn ich mich nicht irre …
2. Was mich betrifft …
3. Um ganz offen zu sein …
4. Übrigens …
5. Es läßt sich nicht leugnen, daß …

b) 1. How shall I put it …
2. I must admit that …
3. Apart from …
4. To come to the point …
5. On the one hand … on the other …

Part 10

1. English is spoken by pilots all over the world.
2. The plane has not been checked.
3. The seat belts must be fastened.
4. Drinks are being served during the flight only.
5. This airport was built ten years ago.

Spelling

Exercise 1

1. really
2. always
3. fulfil
4. awful
5. separate
6. describe
7. character
8. than
9. accept … opinion
10. themselves
11. Another … their
12. believe

Exercise 2

a) 1. sense
2. presence
3. senseless
4. absence
5. sentence
6. accent
7. sensible
8. per cent

Cartoon, p. 12: Down with vowels

Exercise 2

b)	1. proved	4. lose	7. loser
	2. proof	5. losses	8. loss
	3. prove	6. lost	

c)	1. family	4. family-	7. party's
	2. families	5. families'	8. parties
	3. family's	6. party-	9. parties'

d)	1. describes	5. lying	9. weak
	2. display	6. cried	10. Newsweek ... weekly news
	3. divides	7. crying	11. explain ... explanation
	4. died	8. being	12. believe ... belief ... 'F'

e)	1. divide	6. disillusion	11. disintegration
	2. disaster	7. destroy	12. disuse
	3. disinterested	8. disarmament	13. deviation
	4. describe	9. despite	14. dissimilar
	5. despair	10. desegregation	15. divisive factor

Exercise 3

1. answered	5. talks	9. haven't
2. speaks	6. built	10. ---
3. stopped	7. ---	11. cannot
4. ---	8. watches	12. reaches

Exercise 4

a)	1. lives	5. life	9. living
	2. Living	6. life	10. life
	3. life	7. lives	
	4. live	8. live	

b)	1. themselves	3. ourselves	5. selfishness
	2. himself	4. itself	

Revision

Lets consider television and it's development in the next few years. People will discribe it as a 'reinvention of television'. A viewer of the 21st century will not belive that there once where TV sets that merely showed programmes without viewer interaction. As a first step television will establish a new norm (HDTV). This norm will provide more colourfull spectacles and match the quality of motion pictures. An other development will be the optical disc, a brother of the compact disc, that can display photographs, moving video, computer data and printed text. You havn't heard of interactive travelogue discs yet? It is an electronic guide who's range of information is enormous. As the tourist roams through London, for example, he watchs selected programmes and at the same time he can request any information he is intrested in. So, at last, he is realy free to discover London, or other places, on his own. Oppinions on that will, of course, be devided. You can not deny, however, that these are exciting prospects about television in the future. The question is how will we adapt to these rapid changes and there consequences.

Grammar

Article and Determiners

Exercise 1

1. an
2. a
3. a
4. a
5. an
6. a (!)
7. an (!)
8. a ... an
9. an (!)
10. a
11. a (!)
12. a
13. an
14. a
15. an

Exercise 2

a) 1. this
2. these
3. this
4. these
5. this
6. this
7. these
8. these

b) 1. ---
2. These
3. This
4. ---
5. these
6. these
7. ---
8. These

*Exercise 3

a) 1. the
2. --
3. the
4. The
5. --
6. --
7. --
8. the

b) 1. the
2. --
3. --
4. the
5. the

c) 1. the
2. the
3. --
4. The
5. --
6. --

d) 1. --
2. The
3. the
4. the
5. -- ... --
6. --
7. The
8. the
9. the ... --

Adjective vs. Adverb

Exercise 1

a) 1. clear
2. clearly
3. absolutely clear
4. clearly
5. clear
6. clearly
7. clear
8. clearly

b) 1. Normally
2. normal
3. normal
4. Finally ... in a ... way
5. easily
6. easy ... normal

*Exercise 2

1. much greater than
2. extremely difficult person
3. ---
4. the absolute climax
5. peacefully
6. ---
7. many more friends
8. take me seriously
9. are different
10. Most parents

Cartoon, p. 20: "Everybody hang on really tight in case he starts with a sudden jerk!"

*Exercise 3

1. Your answer is clearly wrong.
2. I would like to make that completely clear: it is impossible.
3. His report on the event was very detailed.
4. He reported on the event in a detailed way.
5. He looked at me in a friendly way.
6. There was an old lady who looked very friendly.
7. The author addresses his readers directly.
8. Your proposition is/sounds very unrealistic.

***Exercise 4**

1. well
2. most interesting
3. well ... better
4. easy ... convenient ... more easily
5. more carefully ... most careful
6. worse ... bad ... less good

***Exercise 5**

a) 1. Generally speaking man is a sociable being.
2. That is generally correct.
3. General elections are held every four years.
4. This fact is generally accepted.
5. Generally/In general I get up at 6:30.
6. Hopefully, things will change.
7. Can you give a brief report about the meeting?
8. Briefly speaking, the meeting was cancelled.
9. We will probably have to go there again.
10. This outcome is very probable.

b) 1. What you are saying is simply wrong.
2. She writes in a plain and simple style.
3. Put it as simply as you you can.
4. The text is extremely difficult to understand.
5. He takes an extremely different view.
6. There are extreme differences in their views.
7. The author describes the house in detail.
8. From l. 21 onward he goes into detail.
9. Generally (speaking) that is considered as outdated.
10. The issue is of general interest.
11. That is meant ironically.
12. The title is clearly ironic(al).

Verbs: General

Exercise 1

1. have
2. has
3. has
4. happen
5. is
6. is
7. is
8. is ... say

Exercise 2

1. can be understood
2. is caught
3. chooses
4. ---
5. have you gone
6. has paid off
7. has shown

Exercise 3

1. is faced with
2. is taught
3. Taking
4. needs to feel
5. does not only depend on
6. will develop
7. made ... work
8. cannot
9. hadn't seen
10. he had heard
11. what that meant
12. had not been
13. he could do it ... manage

***Exercise 4**

1. are responsible
2. ---
3. happen
4. is
5. ---
6. ---
7. speaks

***Exercise 5**

admit a), c)
affirm a)
assert a)
assure b)
believe a), b)
confess a), c)
convince b)
explain a), c)
inform b)
mention a), c)
persuade b)
point out a), c)
promise a), b)
remark a), c)
report a), c)
say a), c)
state a), c)
suggest a), c)
tell b)
warn a), b)

Cartoon, p. 24: "This one says it's overpriced."

***Exercise 6**

possible context of situation: holiday / weekend / birthday / family excursion ... planning

1. + that clause / + s.b. of s.th. / + s.b. to do s.th. / + ing-form
2. + s.th. / + ing-form / + that clause
3. + that clause / + on doing s.th.
4. + s.b. to do s.th. / + s.b. that clause

5. + of s.th. / + of doing s.th.
6. + s.b. to do s.th. / + s.th. / + to do s.th.
7. + ing-form / + s.th. / + that clause
8. + (s.b.) that clause / + of s.th. / + s.b. to do s.th.
9. + s.th. to s.b. / + ing-form / + to s.b. how to / + to s.b. that clause
10. + s.b. of s.th. / + s.th. / + s.b. that clause
11. + s.b. about / + s.b. s.th. / + s.b. that clause / + s.b. to do s.th.
12. + that clause / + to s.b. that clause

***Revision**

1. wants to make them understand ... cannot
2. made us leave
3. wanted the young man to plead guilty
4. thought that he had
5. As soon as he arrived home
6. told
7. had waited for
8. is
9. tries
10. aren't afraid
11. aren't allowed
12. used to seeing
13. is sent
14. does not depend
15. is

Verbs: Tenses

***Exercise 1**

a) 1. met
2. did he say
3. said ... had been ... was
4. told ... worried/had worried ... had contracted
5. added ... was ... had recovered
6. had been ... had infected
7. told ... had missed ... had (been asking)/asked
8. had not been ... had happened

b) 1. Tom has been in England. He has learnt his English there.
2. Last week I saw the new scifi film.
3. Our friends have been living in the USA for four years.
They moved there in ...
4. He has been waiting for her for an hour.
He has been standing here since 7 o'clock already.
5. She has left because she had to be at home in time.

6. The money was paid last week already.
   This week we haven't earned anything so far.
7. I have often been asked if I prefer England to the USA.
   I have never thought about it.
8. I haven't understood the difference between the "past" and the "present perfect" yet.

***Exercise 2**

1. will be ... we will have
2. are going to/will find ... is claiming
3. live ... will suffer from
4. A) will be ... is giving
   B) will be/is leaving
   C) is about to leave/is leaving
5. A) Are you getting up ... are you staying
   B) get up ... will be
   C) will feel ... go out
6. A) will be travelling
   B) you go ... will meet/are going to meet
   C) are you going to book
   D) leaves

***Exercise 3**

1. gave you
2. didn't allow
3. we would have reached
4. you tell
5. if children could do
6. She would have come
7. we would have been informed
8. They would have agreed

***Exercise 4**

1. If I were (was) younger, I would study foreign languages.
2. I would become a teacher if teachers were better paid.
3. I would not have begun my studies if I had known they take so long.
4. I would not say that if I did not know it.
5. If you want to be successful in our firm, you will have to work hard.
6. They would certainly have come if we had invited them.
7. If that were right, we would not object to him/disagree.

***Exercise 5**

1. I would certainly make it
2. if I had been more fortunate
3. I'll be most fortunate
4. would ring you up
5. don't agree
6. were/was
7. I had been treated
8. will simply forget

Cartoon, p. 29: "... if he doesn't stop talking, I'll eat him."

**Exercise 6

1. If you look through my binoculars, you can see the mountain tops clearly. You won't be able to see the mountain tops clearly unless you look through my binoculars.
2. You won't see anything unless you look that way. If you don't look that way, you won't see anything.
3. Although we took the binoculars, we couldn't see anything. Despite the fact that we took the binoculars, we couldn't see anything.
4. Although I had the best pair of binoculars, you couldn't see much.
5. I'll let you go home if you leave in silence.
6. Although we tried to leave the building in complete silence, we did not pass unnoticed. We tried to leave the building in complete silence. In spite of that we did not pass unnoticed.
7. If you don't leave now, it might be too late.
8. If you want to leave early tomorrow, let me know this evening. Let me know this evening in case you want to leave early tomorrow.
9. Although I have no idea so far, we'll find a way.
10. Although in the beginning her fears were enormous, she overcame them in the end.

Verbs: Passive Voice

Exercise 1

1. More and more high-rise blocks are built.
2. He has never been accepted as he was.
3. His fears can easily be understood.
4. The kidnapper was tried and condemned.
5. The new sports arena is being built next to the old one I've heard.
6. He is said to be something of an outsider.

*Exercise 2

1. We were shown a film about England.
2. The old man was looked after.
3. I was given an extra premium for my idea.
4. You are considered competent for the job.

5. He is believed to be able to manage.
6. Such a sensation had been unheard of.
7. The meal was paid for by Father.
8. Have you already been offered a position for an apprenticeship?

***Exercise 3**

1. ---
2. had not been checked
3. is to be done
4. was built
5. ---
6. aren't served
7. ---
8. have been invited

***Exercise 4**

1. He had come to see/watch the top match.
2. Unfortunately the match had been cancelled.
3. He really would have liked to watch it.
4. But there wasn't anything to be done at the moment.
5. That had to be accepted.
6. The teams would meet next in two weeks time.
7. He hoped he wouldn't be disappointed again in two weeks time.
8. He had been looking forward to this top match for a month.

Verbs: ing-Form vs. Infinitive

Exercise 1

1. to listen
2. driving ... walking
3. to buy
4. going
5. going(!)
6. to see
7. to be
8. giving
9. taking
10. repeat(!)
11. to get
12. Seeing ... come ... to avoid ... saying

***Exercise 2**

1. to be asked
2. being read
3. being made
4. to be woken ... being left
5. be washed ... peeled ... be consumed
6. being invited ... to be invited
7. being addressed
8. being received

***Exercise 3**

1. travel
2. living
3. speaking
4. walk
5. being
6. work

Miscellaneous

Exercise 1

1. than
2. than
3. than
4. than
5. than
6. than

Cartoon, p. 33: than

*Exercise 2

1. You were late, weren't you?
2. You have not been to the States yet, have you?
3. You often go to the movies, don't you?
4. You do understand what I say, don't you?
5. You saw what happened, didn't you?
6. There wasn't a mistake in the paper, was there?
7. He likes music, doesn't he?
8. You can't possibly come, can you?

*Exercise 3

1. Let us talk about it.
2. He made the students learn a lot of vocabulary.
3. The hit-and-run driver left the injured person lying in the street.
4. My parents let me/allow me to watch as much TV as I want.
5. The customs officer makes us open all our suitcases.
6. Leave us in peace!
7. He had his car washed.
8. What made you change your mind so fast?
9. She left the engine running. She just wanted to post the letter.
10. Take your time.
11. The doctor had the patient taken to hospital.
12. He let/allowed us to go home earlier.

**Exercise 4

1. One ought to/should tell the truth.
2. He is said to have been a famous man.
3. Shall we come a little later today?
4. The text is (meant) to illustrate what I think.
5. You are (supposed) to keep the „papers“ in good care and revise them from time to time.
6. What is that supposed to mean?

7. The reader is meant to be stirred up.
8. The doctor is to come at once.
9. She is said to/is expected to work as a model for 'Vogue'.
10. I ought to/was (supposed) to ring up my parents tonight.

**** Exercise 5**

1. What
2. what
3. which
4. what
5. which
6. what
7. which

Cartoon, p. 36: what

**** Exercise 6**

1. How old are you?
2. What is the name of the English Queen?
3. We should accept people as they are.
4. There is no business like show business.
5. Tell me what she is like in reality.
6. Drive as carefully as you can.
7. How/What about watching TV?
8. The film gives us a good idea of what New York is like.
9. The joke was funny, wasn't it?
10. He told everything as/the way it had happened.

Prepositions

Exercise 1

1. into
2. in ... for ... to
3. At ... on
4. on
5. at ... with
6. with ... in
7. in ... to

Exercise 2

1. by
2. with
3. of ... from
4. by
5. To
6. of/against
7. ---
8. with

Exercise 3

1. by J.D. Salinger
2. ---
3. looks for
4. to stay with
5. ---
6. In contrast to
7. her age
8. agree with me

***Exercise 4**

1. the story by Conan Doyle
2. his attitude towards crime
3. The text reminds me of a film I have seen.
4. Sherlock Holmes looks for the murderer.
5. The magnifying-glass is characteristic of him.
6. The detective concentrates on/focuses on the the offender's motive.
7. Do you remember 'The Hound of the Baskervilles'?
8. Do you believe that criminals think of the possible punishment before their deed?

***Exercise 5**

1. to
2. ---
3. with
4. to
5. on
6. ---
7. to
8. with
9. on
10. to ... by

***Exercise 6**

1. by George Orwell
2. characteristic of
3. ---
4. ---
5. react to
6. ---
7. To O'Brien's mind ... into the society
8. ---

Cartoon, p. 41: "Of course, ...it's only up and down, ...on the somersault."

***Exercise 7**

1. by
2. on
3. of
4. at
5. of
6. ---
7. from
8. of
9. ---
10. into
11. of
12. compared to
13. to
14. with
15. on

***Exercise 8**

1. from
2. of ... of
3. From
4. from
5. of
6. from
7. from
8. of

*Exercise 9

1. The dinner at our friends' was very good.
2. With me that is something different.
3. In detective stories much depends on the solution.
4. We arrived at sunset.
5. Upon closer examination that becomes clear.
6. In our holidays we were near Bordeaux.
7. I work for McDonald's.
8. In traffic situations you must be careful with older people.
9. I can stay with my friends.
10. She took him by the hand.

*Exercise 10

a) 1. to s.b./of
2. for
3. of
4. of
5. for s.th./ to s.b.
6. of
7. for
8. of
9. to
10. for
11. of

b) 1. … to go
2. … of going
3. … from going
4. … against going
5. … to go
6. … to go
7. … go
8. … from going

*Exercise 11

1. Through/Because of the rain the road was impassable.
2. He jumped through the window.
3. He proves his thesis by means of/through examples.
4. America was discovered by the Vikings.
5. As a result of/Because of/Owing to his driving we had an accident.
6. The man was arrested by the police.
7. By changing/Because of our changing the lane we got into trouble.

**Exercise 12

1. in the face of
2. by means of/through
3. With
4. considering/compared to
5. In view of
6. Thanks to/Owing to

**Exercise 13

1. Except for the referee everybody was furious.
2. This development is in line with the latest fashion.
3. In view of the fact that he possibly lies/tells a lie we must listen carefully.

4. According to the doctor he was shot.
5. In relation to the costs of living the wages are low.
6. Owing to the taxidrivers' strike we missed the flight.
7. Along with thousands of others we left the area.
8. As for our 'Kursarbeit' I am going to inform you tomorrow.
9. The candidate defeated his rival by means of a dirty campaign.

***Revision**

1. by
2. of
3. towards
4. of ... by
5. of
6. of
7. for
8. From ... of
9. --- ... of
10. for
11. to
12. of ... in ... of
13. on
14. in
15. on
16. in
17. ---
18. from

Vocabulary

General

Exercise 1

1. typical of (!)
2. happy
3. opinion
4. In contrast to
5. there are/we can observe/we can find
6. make clear <u>to</u> him/make him understand

Exercise 2

1. At last/Eventually/In the end
2. certain/convinced ... cope with/manage
3. In my opinion/As I see it
4. is considered/is known as
5. becomes evident/apparent
6. support that/give proof
7. we find/we observe ... obvious
8. grows/increases
9. diminishes/decreases
10. improving

Exercise 3

a)
1. In contrast to
2. there is/he has
3. proof
4. looks/appearance
5. not ... either
6. argues

b)
1. the worst time
2. reminded her
3. she is able to/she is capable of standing
4. While
5. innocence
6. hardly any
7. desperate

Exercise 4

1. On the one hand ... on the other
2. describes ... in detail
3. While
4. be given
5. depends on
6. he enjoys
7. gives/provides
8. his own opinion
9. addresses ... directly
10. achieves
11. reacts to
12. take ... seriously
13. individual
14. monotonous
15. is meant to/is intended to

***Exercise 5**

1. advantages
2. has fallen/has decreased
3. to avoid/to prevent
4. links/connects
5. employs/uses
6. is (meant) to/is supposed to
7. to climb socially/ to rise on the social ladder
8. to form/to create
9. deal with/cope with
10. arise/crop up

***Exercise 6**

1. It is true ... but
2. means/intends to point out
3. meaningless/pointless ... meaningful/makes sense
4. not perfect/not without a flaw
5. have/go through
6. an opinion of her own
7. Using/The use of ... suggests the idea
8. If I remember correctly/If my memory serves me right
9. There is no denying
10. I dare say/I venture to say
11. among other things
12. Apart from
13. Hence follows/Consequently

14. is said to be/is believed to be
15. totalitarian
16. individuals
17. are to/are expected to
18. applies/uses
19. among
20. wants the people to

***Exercise 7**

1. wenn ich mich recht erinnere/
   wenn mich mein Gedächtnis nicht im Stich läßt
2. abgesehen davon
3. was mich betrifft
4. unter anderem
5. ich möchte Ihnen widersprechen
6. was hier ins Auge fällt, ist
7. es läßt sich argumentieren, daß
8. es ist wichtig, zu unterscheiden zwischen
9. übrigens
10. daraus folgt, daß
11. ich möchte es so ausdrücken
12. es läßt sich nicht leugnen, daß
13. wenn ich mich recht erinnere
14. ich darf wohl sagen
15. abgesehen von

***Exercise 8**

1. strikes me as
2. While
3. hardly any
4. Taking everything into account
5. From my point of view
6. committed herself to/got involved in
7. resigned himself/submitted to his fate
8. suggests/implies
9. can be proved/can be substantiated/is illustrated
10. there are/you can meet/you can find
11. learned/got to know
12. marked by/characterized by
13. can be put down to/can be attributed to
14. admit/confess
15. nowadays/in these days ... in the days of old

***Exercise 9**

1. many jobs
2. to choose
3. we must test
4. point of criticism
5. in detail/in a detailed way
6. has ... work for him
7. inhuman behaviour
8. conceptions of life going on
9. as a consequence of
10. It becomes apparent
11. impersonal behaviour
12. It is paradoxical/It is a paradox
13. advances/puts forth

***Exercise 10**

1. can be proved/can be traced
2. becomes apparent/is revealed
3. runs as follows/is the following
4. there is/we can observe/we can recognize
5. suggests/implies
6. focuses on/is centred on/is centred around
7. reflects/mirrors
8. forms/constitutes/can be considered as
9. is rich in/abounds in
10. at the very beginning ... at the very end
11. urgent/pressing
12. striking/remarkable/outstanding
13. realizes/becomes aware of
14. behave differently from
15. self-realization ... find oneself
16. are worried/are concerned about

****Exercise 11**

1. is (meant)
2. settle/resolve
3. complex/intricate
4. convey/make us see/make us understand
5. can be explained by/can be attributed to
6. articulate/voice/vent
7. depreciatory/derogatory
8. speech/use of English
9. In brief/Briefly/All things considered/To sum it up
10. Frankly speaking/To cut a long story short
11. marked by/is rich in/abounds in/contains a lot of
12. beside the point/out of place
13. I'm uncertain/I'm rather in two minds/I can't make up my mind/I wonder

14. got involved in/joined the
15. triggered/started
16. Undeniably/There is no denying that/I'm quite certain that

Cartoon, p. 56: self-assured

**Exercise 12

1. I'm afraid
2. object/contend
3. can be attributed to/results from
4. is sent to
5. belongs to
6. vicious circle
7. advantages/good side to it
8. self-confidence/self-assurance/self-assertion
9. find herself/find her identity
10. presumption/self-conceit/he has an exaggerated opinion of himself
11. self-evident/That goes without saying

**Exercise 13

a)
1. class disparities/class barriers in Great Britain
2. to feel inwardly superior
3. to suffer from an inferiority complex
4. to pursue a goal/aim/an objective
5. to strive for a socially higher position
6. to adapt to social norms/conventions/to submit to ...
7. to be discriminated against by class prejudice/bias
8. to improve one's social position/one's lot
9. to overcome class barriers
10. to be socially underprivileged

b)
1. unfavourable/underprivileged
2. lower
3. to be unaware of/to be ignorant of
4. to narrow/to bridge
5. to climb up
6. to adapt to/to accept/to conform to
7. to resign oneself
8. below one's rank
9. feel inferior to
10. to achieve the goal

**Exercise 14

1. self-complacent/smug
2. unselfish/self-sacrificing
3. self-esteem/self-respect
4. come true/materialize
5. on the part of
6. pull his weight/be up to his job/meet the demands of his job
7. revolve around/are centred around/focus on
8. is based on/is dependent on/results from

**Exercise 15

1. assertion/allegation
2. examine/deal with/consider
3. moving/touching/impressive
4. striking/remarkable
5. is accurate/represents reality
6. learns/knows from experience/discovers
7. keeps to/limits himself to
8. controversial/contentious
9. contrasts with/is very much opposed to
10. does not exist/is non-existent
11. asserts/claims/observes/states
12. criticizes about
13. contributes to/reinforces/supports
14. creates/brings about/produces the effect of

Word Formation

Exercise 1

a)
1. un-
2. im-
3. in-
4. un-
5. dis-
6. ab-
7. in-
8. im-
9. in-
10. un-

b)
1. dis-
2. mis-
3. in-
4. non-
5. mis-
6. non-
7. dis-
8. in-
9. dis-
10. dis-

Exercise 2

1. to introduce
2. to conclude
3. to interpret
4. to quote
5. to enumerate
6. to argue
7. to assume
8. to explain
9. to juxtapose
10. to solve

Exercise 3

1. argument/argumentation
2. assumption
3. solution of
4. explanation
5. proof
6. indication
7. criticism/critic
8. influence
9. reference
10. inference

Exercise 4

1. portrays
2. lived
3. advises
4. experimental
5. addition
6. basis
7. successive
8. unintentionally ... intentional

Exercise 5

a)

friendship; stardom; childhood; gladness; idealism; membership; arrangement; consideration; adulthood; capitalism; dictatorship; kingdom; astonishment; implication; christianity; weakness; disappointment; relationship; manhood; criticism; confrontation; collection; assumption; advertisement; partnership; freedom; materialism; excitement; kindness

b)

(un)acceptable; childless; childlike; senseless; sensitive; sensible; peaceful; peacelike; peaceable; (un)communicative; literal; spontaneous; figurative; meaningful; meaningless; dangerous; (in)visible; habitual; (un)changeable; (ir)responsible; Elizabethan; capable; (in)active; usual; Victorian; harmful; harmless; (ir)religious; persuasive; Georgian; dreamless; dreamlike; dreamy; useful; useless; lengthy; businesslike; mechanical

False Friends

Exercise 1

a)
1. meaning
2. opinion
3. meaning
4. meaning
5. opinion
6. Opinions
7. meaning
8. opinion

b)
1. remind
2. reminds
3. remember
4. remember
5. reminds
6. remember
7. remind
8. Remember

c)
1. interested
2. interesting
3. interesting
4. interested
5. interesting
6. interested
7. interesting/interested

d)
1. say … said
2. told … told
3. say
4. says … tell … told
5. tells … tell
6. says … say
7. says … tell

e)
1. done
2. made
3. do
4. make
5. do
6. done/made
7. made
8. doing
9. do … make

*Exercise 2

a)
1. Let
2. leave
3. leave
4. let
5. let
6. let
7. leave
8. leave
9. Let's leave

b)
1. news
2. new
3. news
4. news item
5. new
6. news
7. new … news

Cartoon, p. 65: "Bad news, …"

*Exercise 3

1. Can you see what I mean?
2. Do you often watch soap operas?
3. No matter how you look at it, it's hopeless.
4. Look over there, please: what can you see?
5. I wanted to look away but I could not but see the accident.

6. Have you seen the film in which the hero always watches birds?
7. Looking back to my childhood I see now that watching 'Sesame Street' hasn't helped me a bit.

Cartoon, p. 65: possible solution: "Look, Mr Smith, I still don't see the point."

*Exercise 4

1. raise ... rise ... raising ... -rise
2. actual ... topical ... topical
3. finished ... ready ... ready ... finished
4. hardly any ... nearly ... hardly anymore ... nearly
5. at least ... at last ... at least ... at last
6. effect ... affected ... affect ... -effect
7. excited ... exciting
8. hardly ... hard
9. except ... accepted
10. Who's ... whose
11. involved ... engaged
12. realize ... put in practice
13. lying ... laid ... lay
14. adopted ... adapt
15. fewer ... less ... less and less
16. eventually ... possibly
17. sensitive ... sensible
18. self-conscious ... self-confident
19. loose ... losing
20. flee ... fly
21. economic ... economical
22. human ... humane
23. critic ... criticism
24. nice ... sympathetic

**Exercise 5

1. I'd like to give you some good advice.
2. Before he left, he gave his friend some useful advice.
3. I don't expect any advice, I must get along myself.
4. We received a lot of important information.
5. Can you give me information on the British education(al) system?

**** Exercise 6**

1. Politics is a difficult matter.
2. Politicians choose the people in their immediate surroundings carefully.
3. Which information and factual evidence can be provided to support the President's thesis?
4. The audience is/viewers are very interested in learning that from the mass media.
5. Demonstrations are a peaceful means of protest.
6. After various crises the USA made good progress in their negotiations with the USSR.

*** Revision**

a) 1. Sie ist eine sehr mitfühlende Person. (nice = sympathisch)
2. Wenn er zu sehr unter Druck steht, kann er schließlich zusammenbrechen (perhaps; possibly = vielleicht; eventuell)
3. Deutschland läßt die englische Mannschaft schlagen. (has beaten = hat geschlagen)
4. Er ist der gewöhnlichste Typ, den ich kenne. (primitive; rude = ordinär)
5. Hast du je jemanden getroffen, der schüchterner war als mein Freund (self-confident; self-assured = selbstsicher)
6. Jeder sagt, sie sei ein vernünftiges Mädchen (sensitive = empfindsam; sensibel)

b) 1. to take a seat/to sit down
2. to take place
3. no ... either
4. ingenious/outstanding
5. colloquial
6. meaningful/a sensible answer/makes sense
7. traced/observed

c) 1. He has no opinion of his own.
2. In contrast to me you have a job.
3. We are sure this day will make you happy.
4. There is no decisive difference.
5. I am going to explain the reason in detail.
6. Her life circumstances are simply inhuman.
7. You receive your gift today already.
8. The text can be divided into three main sections.
9. The ad is meant to/was conceived to manipulate the consumers' attitude/habits.
10. The text reminds me of a film which I have seen.

11. In the introductory part/In the introduction he presents his topic.
12. In the main part he provides a lot of facts.
13. That is typical of you: You'll never admit anything.
14. The author argues in a one-sided way.
15. The author argues consistently.

Text Analysis and Text Production

Exercise 1

1. Ein auffälliges Beispiel für ... erscheint in Zeile 20.
2. In den Zeilen ... führt der Autor aus, daß ...
3. Das wird deutlich in den Zeilen ..., in denen der Autor sich auf ... bezieht.
4. Das Wort/Der Satz in Zeile ... legt nahe, daß/bedeutet, daß ...
5. Das läßt sich nachweisen in den Zeilen ...
6. Ein Beweis für .../dafür läßt sich in den Zeilen ... finden.

Exercise 2

1. falls into/breaks into
2. comprises
3. extends from ... to
4. As a first step
5. constitutes
6. eventually/at last

Exercise 3

1. is concerned with/deals with
2. meets with/is faced with
3. assumes
4. emphasizes/supports
5. result in/end in
6. brings about/creates
7. intends to say/maintains/assumes
8. provide
9. is convinced that/believes/supposes/asserts
10. illustrates/demonstrates that
11. is concerned with/tackles
12. is rich in/abounds in
13. uses/employs/includes
14. avoids/refrains from/sticks to objectivity

*Exercise 4

a) statement

<table>
<tr><td rowspan="11">Der</td><td rowspan="11">Autor
Sprecher</td><td colspan="2">sagt aus,</td><td rowspan="10">daß …</td></tr>
<tr><td colspan="2">versichert,</td></tr>
<tr><td colspan="2">erklärt,</td></tr>
<tr><td colspan="2">bestätigt,</td></tr>
<tr><td colspan="2">nimmt an,</td></tr>
<tr><td colspan="2">impliziert,</td></tr>
<tr><td colspan="2">führt aus,</td></tr>
<tr><td colspan="2">sagt abschließend,</td></tr>
<tr><td colspan="2">folgert,</td></tr>
<tr><td>versucht</td><td>zu zeigen,
zu beweisen,</td></tr>
<tr><td colspan="3">versucht, den Leser zu überzeugen.</td></tr>
</table>

b) structure

<table>
<tr><td rowspan="8">Der</td><td rowspan="8">Autor
Sprecher</td><td>entwickelt …</td></tr>
<tr><td>ordnet …</td></tr>
<tr><td>arrangiert …</td></tr>
<tr><td>vergleicht …</td></tr>
<tr><td>kontrastiert …</td></tr>
<tr><td>stellt nebeneinander …</td></tr>
<tr><td>hält auseinander …</td></tr>
<tr><td>zieht einen analogen Vergleich …</td></tr>
</table>

c) neutral attitude

<table>
<tr><td rowspan="3">Der</td><td rowspan="3">Autor</td><td>versucht, neutral zu bleiben bei …</td></tr>
<tr><td>nimmt eine neutrale Haltung ein zu …</td></tr>
<tr><td>ergreift keine Partei für …</td></tr>
</table>

d) positive attitude

<table>
<tr><td rowspan="7">Der</td><td rowspan="7">Autor
Sprecher</td><td>verteidigt das Argument, daß …</td></tr>
<tr><td>ist überzeugt von der Tatsache, daß …</td></tr>
<tr><td>unterstützt die Idee, daß …</td></tr>
<tr><td>pflichtet der Tatsache bei, daß …</td></tr>
<tr><td>unterstreicht die Vorstellung, daß …</td></tr>
<tr><td>ist der Auffassung, daß …</td></tr>
<tr><td>ist begeistert von …</td></tr>
</table>

e) argument

Er	kritisiert, daß ... greift die Vorstellung, daß ..., an. stellt die Tatsachen, daß ..., in Frage. macht die Vorstellung lächerlich, daß ... warnt vor einer Entwicklung, die ... könnte. nimmt nicht ernst, daß ... bringt seine Zweifel zum Ausdruck, daß ... übertreibt, wenn er sagt, daß ...

**Exercise 5

1. goes into particulars/illustrates his view by means of examples/provides a lot of illustrative (concrete) detail
2. remains on an abstract level/argues abstractly/tends to abstract argumentation
3. supplies definite (precise/exact) data on/gives substantial information on
4. In terms of facts/Put in concrete terms
5. as for example/as for instance/such as
6. provides/furnishes/gives
7. If you take ... for example/for instance
8. Other (Further) examples (instances) of

**Exercise 6

optimistic	= optimistisch	pessimistic	= pessimistisch
bright	= klug, intelligent	dull slow	= dumm, unintelligent
law-abiding	= gesetzestreu	disobedient	= ungehorsam
unselfish	= selbstlos	selfish	= selbstsüchtig
assertive	= anspruchsvoll, anmaßend	timid	= schüchtern
		shy	= scheu
strong-willed	= willensstark	weak-willed	= willensschwach
unassuming	= anspruchslos	self-complacent	= selbstgefällig
reliable	= verläßlich	unreliable	= unzuverlässig
dynamic	= dynamisch	static	= statisch
regardful	= aufmerksam, rücksichtsvoll	regardless	= rücksichtslos
		thoughtless	= unbesonnen
tolerant	= tolerant	intolerant	= intolerant
sympathetic	= mitfühlend		
considerate	= rücksichtsvoll	inconsiderate	= rücksichtslos
elevated	= erheitert	depressed	= niedergeschlagen

sociable	= gesellig	unsociable	= ungesellig
		secluded	= zurückgezogen
grateful	= dankbar	ungrateful	= undankbar
conscientious	= gewissenhaft	superficial	= oberflächlich
confiding	= vertrauensvoll	suspicious	= mißtrauisch
trustful	= vertrauensvoll		
intimate	= vertraut, intim	aloof	= distanziert
tough	= hart	soft	= weich
tactful	= taktvoll	tactless	= taktlos
		rude	= grob
broad-minded	= großzügig	narrow-minded	= engstirnig
		stupid	= töricht
self-centred	= ichbezogen	altruistic	= uneigennützig
irresponsible	= verantwortungslos	responsible	= verantwortungsvoll

**Exercise 7

a) 1. Der Autor lenkt die Aufmerksamkeit des Lesers auf …
2. Der Autor appelliert an die Gefühle des Lesers.
3. Der Autor erregt das Interesse/stimuliert die Vorstellungskraft … des Lesers.
4. Der Autor versucht, die Haltung des Lesers zu verändern/ zu beeinflussen …
5. Der Text/Das Argument ruft beim Leser eine Reaktion hervor/ bewirkt eine Reaktion beim Leser.

b) 1. nämlich
2. mit (in) anderen Worten
3. d.h.
4. Anders ausgedrückt
5. Um es einfacher zu sagen
6. oder eher/besser

Exercise 8

1. can be divided into/falls/breaks into
2. extends from … to/reaches from … to
3. begins … ends
4. comprises
5. As a first step/To begin with
6. goes on to/proceeds to
7. contains/can be considered as

Exercise 9

a) Zu Beginn …

führt		Thema	
präsentiert	der Autor seine	These	(ein).
nennt		Hauptgedanken	

	beginnt, indem er klarstellt, daß …
Der Autor	zitiert …
	weist zurück/widerlegt …

b) In der Folge …
entwickelt der Autor seine Gedanken.

	gliedert	… in Hauptschritten.
	baut auf	
Er	geht in Einzelheiten.	
	zählt … Beispiele von … auf.	
	beschränkt sich auf …	
	stellt … gegenüber/kontrastiert …	
	wägt das Für und Wider von … ab.	

c) Schließlich …
beschließt der Autor seinen Gedankengang.

	sagt abschließend …
	zieht die Schlußfolgerung, indem er sagt …
Er	kehrt zum Anfang zurück, indem er sagt …
	unterstreicht …
	betont abschließend …

Exercise 10

Es ist oft gesagt worden, daß …
Man sagt häufig, daß …
Der Autor behauptet, daß …

Nun, dies ist einfach unwahr.
Nun, er/sie hat eindeutig Unrecht darin.
Offengesagt, das ist Unsinn!

Zum einen läßt sich nicht leugnen, daß …
Zunächst ist unbestreitbar, daß …
Einerseits verwirrt es mich, daß …

Zum anderen sieht er nicht, daß ...
Zweitens übersieht er, daß ...

Im übrigen muß man berücksichtigen, daß ...
Drittens sagt mir die eigene Erfahrung, daß ...

Daher will mir scheinen, daß ...
Alles zusammen betrachtet ...
Wenn ich alles in Betracht ziehe, denke ich, daß ...

Ich bin ganz auf ... Seite, wenn es darum geht, daß ...

Collocations

*Exercise 1

1. subdivide/break
2. taking/looking at
3. make up
4. achieve/pursue
5. come to/speak to
6. cope with
7. assumes/adopts
8. follows/appears
9. arises/must be posed

*Exercise 2

1. Hence it follows that
2. As far as I am concerned
3. That is to say
4. As it appears to me
5. What is more
6. As a first step
7. From my point of view
8. Taking everything into consideration

**Exercise 3

1. advance/put forth
2. find/hit upon
3. give/provide
4. exercise/exert
5. draw
6. make
7. give/provide
8. assume/adopt

*Exercise 4

1. sum/brief
2. long story
3. In
4. whole
5. all
6. nutshell
7. considered

****Exercise 5**

1. draws
2. can serve as/can be considered as
3. fulfills
4. is seen as/constitutes
5. deserves/merits
6. is faced with/is confronted with
7. has had/has gone through

****Exercise 6**

1. deeply/profoundly
2. flatly/completely
3. vaguely
4. bitterly/grimly
5. vividly
6. precisely/accurately

****Exercise 7**

1. great/considerable/prime/vital/utmost
2. little/slight/minor/secondary
3. reasonable/sensible
4. vivid
5. close/intimate
6. strained/tensed-up
7. have in common/share
8. decently/with respect/with dignity

****Exercise 8**

1. quote
2. refer
3. evolve
4. present/develop/put forth/defend
5. enlarges on/expands/elaborates
6. arrive at/come to
7. begins/continues/ends
8. goes
9. draws
10. contrasts/compares/juxtaposes
11. relies on/is based on
12. carry ... stand ... are
13. employs/makes use of/resorts to ... to support/to corroborate
14. makes/sees
15. reveals/shows

**** Exercise 9**

1. (+) conclusive/convincing/plausible
   (–) inconclusive/unconvincing/implausible
2. (+) sharp/striking
   (–) slight/hardly noticeable
3. (+) show/display/reveal ... openly
   (–) hide/disguise/cover up/control
4. (+) at home/at ease/optimistic/confident/comfortable
   (–) tensed-up/uncomfortable/ill at ease/depressed/pessimistic
5. (+) in detail/precisely/accurately/vividly
   (–) at great length/vaguely/boringly/insufficiently/imprecisely

**** Exercise 10**

a) 1. mail/goods/a speech/a statement
2. a glass/the voice/trouble/objection/a question/money/a complaint
3. a cause/a view
4. a thesis/a policy/a scheme/a plan
5. an argument/a thesis/a proposal/a proposition

b) 1. miss/achieve/struggle for/fight for/pursue/set up
2. fulfil/perform/carry out
3. give/provide/collect/produce/come up with
4. take/assume/adopt
5. have/go through/speak from

**** Exercise 11**

a) 1. reveals/shows
2. describes/depicts/portrays/characterizes
3. carries weight ... stands
4. come to/draw/arrive at/reach
5. begins/ends

b) 1. urgent/pressing/current/serious/grave/complicated/intricate
2. slight/insignificant/striking/great
3. holds/shares/takes/presents/puts forth/advocates
4. apt/suitable/appropriate/varied/skilful/few/inappropriate
5. serious/gnawing/no/not the least/not the slightest
6. have/exert/exercise/are under
7. plausible/solid/apparent/compelling/obvious/important/feeble

****Exercise 12**

1. to
2. with
3. to
4. on
5. on
6. to
7. about
8. with
9. of
10. at
11. at
12. on
13. to
14. of
15. to

****Exercise 13**

1. expressly
2. increasingly
3. completely/utterly
4. deeply/greatly
5. strongly/highly/fully
6. object strongly/violently ... extremely

Some Thematic Fields

***Exercise 1**

a) conjunction

While/whereas my friend left our school, I stayed on and passed my 'A' levels.
My first girl-friend had blonde hair while my present one has dark hair.

adverbials

On the one hand a majority favours German unification on the other most people are not willing to sacrifice much for it.
Most Germans favour German unification. Yet hardly anybody is willing to pay higher taxes for it.
German unification will take some years to be completed. Most East Germans, however, are not patient enough to wait any longer.
Our friends and allies are concerned about security in Europe. They support the German people in their will to unify their country, though.

prepositions

Unlike North and South Korea, the two Germanys will be unified in due time.
In contrast to the U.S. government, the Soviets still believe that unified Germany cannot be a ful member in the NATO.

b)

etwas bildet einen	leichten unmerklichen direkten scharfen klar erkennbaren auffälligen	Kontrast oder Gegensatz zu …

es gibt einen offensichtlichen Gegensatz zu …
etwas ist das genaue Gegenteil von etwas anderem
… ist/sind sehr verschieden voneinander.
… sind sehr gegensätzlich/unterschiedlich.

c) 1. in contrast to/in opposition to
2. however
3. while/whereas
4. sharp/striking/an obvious contrast
5. very different indeed/differ very much
6. Unlike/Contrary to
7. the very antithesis of/the very opposite of
8. On the one hand … on the other

*Exercise 2

a) ein Argument vorbringen
einem Argument zustimmen

ein Argument	zurückweisen diskutieren betrachten, erwägen

über ein Argument nachdenken

b)

stichhaltig wirkungsvoll begründet zwingend sachdienlich unangreifbar unbezweifelbar	oder	schwach fragwürdig unzutreffend wacklig nicht stichhaltig schlecht begründet

c) gegen/für etwas argumentieren
mit jemandem diskutieren/sich mit jemandem streiten
die Sache lohnt keine Auseinandersetzung
er erwog das Für und Wider
er argumentierte damit, daß …

***Exercise 3**

a) Unterschiede zwischen Dingen/Leuten/Situationen, etc. können ...

groß markant beträchtlich ernst auffällig wesentlich bedeutsam	oder	leicht unbedeutsam klein fein kaum wahrnehmbar	sein.

b) Der Unterschied liegt in der Tatsache, daß ...
Zwei Dinge/Leute etc. sind so verschieden wie Äpfel und Birnen.
Es macht keinen Unterschied.
Es kommt auf das gleiche hinaus.
Wir haben eine Meinungsverschiedenheit.
Man unterscheidet zwischen ...

****Exercise 4**

1. We haven't had much sleep. For that reason we are in bad shape today.
   As we haven't had much sleep, we are in bad shape today.
   We haven't had much sleep. As a consequence we are in bad shape today.
2. Have you thought of the upcoming class test? That is why I can't go out tonight. One reason that I can't go out tonight is the upcoming class test.
   I can't go out tonight because of the upcoming class test.
3. Air travel is becoming a risk these days. That implies you should think twice before you fly to America.
   Air travel is becoming a risk these days. As a consequence you should think twice before flying to America.
   As air travel is becoming a risk these days, you should think twice before flying to America.
4. The Defence Minister was involved in illegal arms sales. As a consequence he had to resign at once.
   Since the Defence Minister was involved in illegal arms sales, he had to resign at once.
   The Defence Minister was involved in illegal arms sales. That led to his having to resign at once.
5. Our National Health Service is becoming too expensive. That implies that fees have to be raised or the costs of medical treatment have to be brought down.
   Our National Health Service is becoming too expensive so that fees have to be raised or the costs of medical treatment have to be brought down.
   Our National Health Service is becoming too expensive. For that (very) reason

fees have to be raised or the costs of medical treatment have to be brought down.

6. The greenhouse effect will make itself felt within the next 30–50 years. As a consequence the western countries will have to change their way of life.
   Owing to the greenhouse effect, which will make itself felt within the next 30–50 years, the western countries will have to change their way of life.
   As the greenhouse effect will make itself felt within the next 30–50 years, the western countries will have to change their way of life.

** Exercise 5

1. Evidently/Obviously
2. Unfortunately
3. Amazingly
4. No doubt/Doubtlessly
5. Inevitably
6. Strangely enough

Sentences

Word Order

Exercise 1

a) 1. In the story two main characters are presented.
2. You can see this in ll. 20-25.
3. They solve that problem by talking to each other.
4. The author, for example, writes that life is boring.
5. There are some facts necessary to prove this idea.
6. In his text the author discusses a problem of topical interest.
7. With Christmas I associate the idea of snow-covered trees.
8. For many people Christmas means presents and good food.

b) 1. In the end Bob leads the same life as before.
2. Both his parents work and, due to this, they think he should take up a job, too.
3. In the second unit the life that Bob leads after moving out is described.
4. From Bob's side the relationship between parents and son is cool.
5. Bob's parents see an idler, not a son in him.
6. What the family's living conditions are like is also shown.

c) 1. In a mixed ability class all pupils are together.
2. Bright and slow pupils are taught in one class.
3. The living conditions are also improved.

4. In this text the main clauses are predominant.
5. In the whole text only facts are given.

Exercise 2

1. In his book the author discusses ...
2. With New York everybody associates ...
3. That statement you can find ...
4. The author writes, for example, that ...
5. In New York people always visit ...
6. In that book both ... are presented.
7. It is said in the text that ...

Exercise 3

1. In the World State called 'Brave New World' no deep emotions are allowed.
2. The author A. Huxley wrote that book in the 1930ies.
3. ---
4. John has lived in a different world all the years.
5. ---
6. He would try to do everything against the 'Brave New World' state.
7. ---
8. With their spray guns the police pump thick clouds of soma into the air.
9. You can only call this world "Ugly New World".

Adverbial Clauses

Exercise 1

1. As he had a temperature, he went to see the doctor.
   He went to see the doctor because he had a temperature.
   He had a temperature. That is why he went to see the doctor.
2. We have a holiday tomorrow. Therefore we needn't get up early.
   As we have a holiday tomorrow, we needn't get up early.
   We have a holiday tomorrow. That is why we haven't to get up early.
3. It had grown dark already. That is the reason why we couldn't go on.
   Since it had grown dark already, we couldn't go on.
   We couldn't go on because it had grown dark already.
4. You've done a good job today. Consequently you won't have to do any homework.
   Since you've done a good job today, you won't have to do any homework.
   You've done a good job today. Therefore you won't have to do any homework.

5. His temperature has gone down. That is why the doctor said he might get up the following day.
   As his temperature has gone down, the doctor said he might get up the following day.
   The doctor said he might get up the following day because his temperature has gone down.
6. I went home early because the show was a flop.
   As the show was a flop, I went home early.
   The show was a flop. That is why I went home early.

Exercise 2

Possible solutions:
1. My father is bilingual so he decided to take up a job as an interpreter.
2. I took the bus in order to keep my driver's license.
3. Take a taxi to the airport in case the bus drivers are on strike.
4. It was late. He came in silently so as not to disturb the rest of the family.
5. He prepared himself carefully so as to make sure he'd pass the test.
6. He did not take part in the demonstration in order to avoid trouble.
7. I'll remind him again so he won't forget it this time.
8. Why don't we climb to the summit so that we might enjoy the fine view.

***Exercise 3**

1. In spite of their saying 'no'/their refusal ...
2. Although he interpreted ... excellently, ...
3. In spite of the difficulty ...
4. In spite of the film being very long/the film's length ...
5. Despite his knowledge ...
6. Although we complained permanently, ...
7. Although she firmly believed in ghosts, ...
8. In spite of my parent's saying 'yes'/consent ...
9. Although we condemned ...
10. In spite of our proving him wrong/the proof that he was wrong ...

***Exercise 4**

Possible solutions:
1. Although he spends a lot on clothes, he always looks underdressed.
2. In spite of the fact that she doesn't work hard, she passes all her tests brilliantly.
3. My friend has never been to the States, although he has an American accent.
4. Even if he apologizes, I won't forget what he did to me.
5. However hard I tried, I was unable to complete the task.

6. I did not enjoy the meal, although the food was good.
7. Despite the fact that I told him to stay, he departed.

****Exercise 5**

1. on the contrary/instead/conversely
2. yet/all the same/nevertheless/in spite of that
3. however/yet
4. however/yet/at the same time/nevertheless
5. on the contrary/instead/but/by contrast
6. still/yet/in spite of that/nevertheless
7. but/yet/all the same/nevertheless/in spite of that/at the same time

Relative Clauses

Exercise 1

1. Is that the new Mercedes model you pointed out to me the other day?
2. This is the police officer I asked about the way this morning.
3. The policemen <u>who</u> were all very young found it difficult to keep calm.
4. Last year I revisited the place (that) I used to live in for 20 years.
5. Bring me the magazine I left on the table that stands near the window.
6. The problem you were arguing about last night has been settled, which was not an easy job I can tell you.

*Exercise 2

1. Everything he owned was stolen.
2. That only happened the day before, <u>which</u> has annoyed him a lot.
3. His father, <u>who</u> was living upstairs in the house, had been fast asleep.
4. The things he needed most were his passport and his driver's license.
5. His father told <u>what</u> he had seen and heard: nothing, <u>which</u> did not surprise the son at all.
6. <u>Whatever</u> the police tried to make clear to him, he knew that he would not see again <u>what</u> was valuable.

*Exercise 3

a) 1. is the man who
2. whose names
3. who are
4. to fire employees he has known/his employees whom he has known
5. the principle of which

6. All that counts
7. no matter how old he is
8. a job that

b) 1. whom he finds sitting
2. that exploits/who exploits
3. an employee he has known/his employee, whom he has known
4. of which
5. All that counts
6. <u>and</u> it does not matter

Style

*Exercise 1

1. As everybody shouted across the room nobody understood what I wanted to say.
2. When I was crossing the room I ran into her./I ran into her as she was crossing the room.
3. I had the impression that they were all models who were dressed in the latest fashion.
4. The main roads were congested with cars blowing their horns.
5. I deeply regret insulting you.
6. When they had finally arrived we welcomed our friends.
7. As we were afraid of burglars we locked every door and window.
8. Although we had asked more than once for the way we found nobody who could tell us where to go.

*Exercise 2

1. The president tells the CBS correspondent that the tax plan will be announced soon.
2. The president's tax cuts make sense because everybody thinks they are necessary for our country.
3. He stated that every citizen, no matter how much he or she earned, would have to pay more taxes.
4. His aides said that if the higher taxes bothered the taxpayers, the president should cut them.
5. At one time the president was a model student at Harvard, a fact that many people still remember.

6. After studying the speech I regard it as of poor rhetoric.
7. When he tried to ring up his campaign manager, the president dialled the wrong number.

****Exercise 3**

1. Unklarer Bezug; besser: If you read the text for the first time, it seems rather difficult to understand.
2. Doppelte Subordination durch 'that'; besser: I have seen accidents happen so often that I tend to overlook them now.
3. 'Nevertheless' und 'but' nicht zusammen in einem Satz; besser: Besides you can find other highpoints of action, which are not so striking.
4. Unlogische Parallele 'atmosphere' und 'classroom'; besser: The atmosphere in the first part is dark and gloomy. One can compare it with that in the classroom in the other story we read.
5. Unklare Parallele 'ten lines' und 'the author'; besser: In contrast to the first ten lines, which are marked by a general approach to the topic, the following lines contain a detailed description.
6. Satzungetüm, in 2–3 Sätze auflösen; besser: The example implies that nobody is perfect. So he should be forgiven for behaving in the wrong way. This, I believe, is what the author wants to point out.

***Exercise 4**

1. definitely/honestly/frankly/simply
2. certainly/definitely/obviously/badly/more or less/partly/not ... at all/ to some extent/not in the least
3. definitely/obviously/simply/absolutely/completely/entirely/a bit
4. honestly/simply/completely/entirely/more or less
5. honestly/certainly
6. scarcely/barely ... absolutely/simply
7. completely/entirely
8. to some extent/partly
9. definitely/simply/entirely
10. more or less/partly
11. frankly/not ... at all/not in the least
12. certainly/... indeed

***Exercise 5**

1. Es ist wohlbekannt, daß ...
2. Es ist ziemlich unwahrscheinlich, daß ...
3. Ich denke, es ist gerechtfertigt, zu sagen, daß ...
4. Aus oben erwähnten Gründen ...

5. Um es ganz einfach auszudrücken …
6. Die Frage erhebt sich, ob …
7. Laßt uns annehmen, daß …
8. Natürlich/Wie zu erwarten war …
9. Es leuchtet ohne weiteres ein, daß …
10. Wenn man nach … urteilt …
11. Wenn ich mich recht erinnere …
12. Wenn es darum geht, zu …
13. Egal wie/wann/wo/was …
14. Auf die Dauer …
15. Die Tatsache bleibt bestehen, daß …
16. Man kann mit Sicherheit sagen, daß …
17. Es liegt in der Natur der Sache, daß …
18. Merkwürdigerweise …

***Exercise 6**

1. Besides/Furthermore/What is more
2. that is why/therefore/as a result/consequently
3. instead/by contrast/rather/at the same time
4. By the way/Incidentally
5. i.e./That is to say
6. nevertheless/all the same/at the same time

***Exercise 7**

1. not only … but also/neither … nor …
2. both … and …
3. either … or …
4. not … either.
5. as early as …
6. as late/early as …
7. as far as …
8. not … either.
9. The … the …
10. both … and …/neither … nor …

****Exercise 8**

<u>forcefullness</u>

1. The author uses/employs striking metaphors.
2. We were proved wrong/They proved us wrong.
3. The poet portrays the city of Chicago.
4. The author/poet evokes the impression of gloom by means of …
5. I believe/I consider the author's view is/as …
6. In l. 67 the speaker re-establishes …
7. In the main part the author enlarges on …
8. The author presents/outlines the punk movement.

fluency

1. As he worked hard to please his students, he was ...
2. Although he started early and promised the taxi driver an extra tip he did not make it in time. The traffic jam was too heavy.
3. Although she was a popular girl and received countless proposals she decided not to get married for the time being.
4. With an extra premium/Having earned an ... we were able to afford the new car.
5. One can mention that E. Pound uses a rich metaphorical language. The originality of his metaphors makes his text sound very interesting./ The original metaphors E. Pound uses in his poem make it sound quite interesting and fresh.

**** Exercise 9**

concreteness

1. konkretisieren!
2. He behaves in an unfriendly way ...
3. 'A' and 'B' differ in that they ... (konkretisieren!)
4. The relationship is strained, disturbed, marked by indifference, etc.
5. ... describes the main character as arrogant, conceited, ruthless, aggressive inconsiderate, unreliable, etc. (konkretisieren!)

precision

1. ... begins by ... and ends by ...
2. The conclusion can be found ...
3. Throughout the text ...
4. You get the impression of a discussion between author and reader.
5. The ideas just mentioned/These ideas ...
6. The author deals with the question of when to ...
7. According to him/In his opinion ...

**** Exercise 10**

1. The image in l. 12 suggests not only his ... but also his ...
2. ... are swimming, surfing and lying on the beach.
3. What he said and what he meant was not the same.
4. He praised both the food and the accommodation.
5. By examining ... and by studying ... you can establish ...
6. ... explains the present situation and expresses his conviction that ...

** Exercise 11

<u>end-focus</u>

1. World War II was won by ...
2. Cancer is caused, among other things, by smoking.
3. America was discovered by Norsemen ...

<u>contrastive focus</u>

1. ... not white wine ...
2. ... not in the north ...
3. ... rather than a human mind/brain ...
4. ... being lazy ...

<u>cleavage</u>

1. It is the sports channel I want to watch.
2. It is because it raised many questions that ...
3. It is after the Joneses left that ...
4. It was | the class speaker who ... / this incident that ... / to the head master that ...

** Exercise 12

a) 1. learn/come to know
2. to contact s.b./establish contact with
3. becomes
4. we begin to understand better

b) 1. The author is concerned with/presents
2. She believes/is convinced that we must act now.
3. He tries to justify chemical warfare.
4. In his articles he portrays/describes Britain in the nineties.

** Exercise 13

1. introduces and confirm<u>s</u>
2. strives to write and <u>uses</u>
3. we have gone ... and that we must think of ...
4. Everyone of us ... their flight tickets
5. have ... and win ...
6. point ... <u>is</u> the fees

Revision Test 1

Part 1

1. is revealed
2. no ... either
3. inconsistent
4. infer/conclude
5. maintains/claims
6. it is significant/important to distinguish between
7. want you to
8. is to
9. essential/significant
10. It is true ...

Part 2

1. of
2. of
3. To
4. ---
5. towards
6. to
7. to
8. on
9. of/against
10. against

Part 3

1. Do you often watch soap operas on TV?
2. Look (over) there! What can you see?
3. I tried to look away but I could not help watching the accident.
4. For this report we need a lot of information.
5. Let me give you some advice.

Part 4

1. lose
2. relative
3. believe
4. divided
5. being
6. themselves
7. practise
8. business
9. proof
10. explanation

Part 5

1. conclusion
2. pros ... cons
3. bridge/close
4. born
5. account/consideration
6. of her own
7. evidence
8. puts forth/advances
9. more
10. achieved

Part 6

1. Our Englishman has been living with us in Germany for 10 years.
2. Last year he spent his vacation in the U.K.
3. He has often been in Spain, too.

4. If you asked him, he would say his favourite country was Spain.
5. He has often been asked how he likes Germany.
6. If he were a German, he would want to live nowhere else.
7. He has tried/been trying for years to get a well-paid job in Spain.
8. He would have had a job there for some time if he had learned Spanish.
9. Last month he went to Spain again.
10. If he is very fortunate, he may/will be able to work in Spain next year.

Part 7

1. In his mind the problem of hunger in the world can easily be solved.
2. That is also my idea about it.
3. In the northern hemisphere the wealthy nations are to be found.
4. The hunger problem can only be solved on a worldwide scale.
5. All over the world there are/exist nations who have enough to eat.

Part 8

1. arise
2. significant
3. juxtaposes
4. emphasizes
5. enumerates
6. result in
7. confronted with
8. take/adopt
9. collected/had
10. As I see it, ...

Part 9

1. That is what I wanted to know.
2. Her coming, which nobody had expected, was the sensation.
3. The entire money was gone, which surprised nobody.
4. He did what he could to help us.
5. She has a reason for her absence, which lets everything appear in a different light.

Revision Test 2

Part 1

1. explained to us
2. We thought (that) we were able to ...
3. He was looking forward to meeting ...
4. made him answer
5. get used to eating

Part 2

1. to cut a long story short .../the long and short of it is ...
2. (all) in all; in sum ...
3. a convincing/cogent argument
4. to refute/reject an argument
5. doubtless/there can be no doubt ...
6. the question arises if/may be posed if ...
7. judging by ...
8. he is inclined to believe .../he takes the view that ...
9. to picture s.th. vividly
10. to take s.th. for granted

Part 3

1. ---
2. --- ... ---
3. the ... the
4. the ... --- ... ---
5. The ... the

Part 4

1. insignificant/slight/small
2. relaxed/easy-going
3. defends/endorses/supports
4. Nowadays things are different.
5. denies
6. I wonder/I suspect/I'm not sure if
7. perhaps
8. ill-founded/beside the point
9. hid/disguised

Part 5

a) 1. That is a clear sign <u>of</u> your intolerance.
2. Queuing is typical <u>of</u> the British.

b) 1. Tell me <u>what</u> windsurfing is really <u>like.</u>
2. The story was absolutely boring, <u>wasn't it?</u>
3. <u>As</u> I see it there is no way out.

Part 6

1. He has completed/finished his work.
2. Bad news is good news.
3. That is a question of topical interest.
4. He has hardly any chance.
5. We have at least given our best.

Part 7

1. in contrast to
2. puts forth
3. paradoxical
4. maintains

5. deserves
6. serve
7. present
8. point of criticism
9. makes sense/is sensible
10. does not matter

Part 8

1. Are you going to come next week?
2. He leaves tomorrow morning at 6:15.
3. Next month he will be sunbathing in Spain.
4. It is going to rain in a minute.
5. It will be sunny everywhere tomorrow.

Part 9

1. chalk and cheese
2. deeply/profoundly
3. the fact
4. short of it is
5. reasons
6. reason
7. done
8. ask
9. pros and cons
10. certain

Part 10

1. consequences
2. test
3. leave ... open
4. accept
5. sensible

Revision Test 3

Part 1

1. choice
2. referring
3. disillusion
4. describes
5. proof

Part 2

1. Whose book have you got there?
2. the problem and its solution
3. Could you possibly come tomorrow?
4. He is very self-assured/self-confident.
5. She is a nice/likeable person.
6. That is not correct either.
7. Do you do your homework?
8. The author remains on an abstract level.
9. He has committed himself to Greenpeace.

Part 3

a) 1. with
2. near
3. at

b) 1. Because of
2. by
3. by means of

c) 1. In view of
2. according to
3. compared to/ in relation to
4. owing to

Part 4

1. indirectly
2. Implicitly
3. indirect
4. well-
5. vividly

Part 5

1. device
2. employs
3. is/becomes aware of
4. urgent
5. strained
6. can be traced
7. makes us understand
8. has affected
9. be blamed for
10. restricts himself from/ refrains from using concrete terms

Part 6

1. criticism
2. provides
3. sensitive
4. advantages
5. leave
6. accept
7. excited
8. adapt to
9. is supposed to

Part 7

1. the nature
2. takes/adopts/assumes
3. needless
4. detail
5. conviction
6. has it
7. convincing (+); ill-founded (–)
8. striking (+); slight (–)

Part 8

1. One can distinguish between ...
2. It can be argued that .../One can maintain that ...
3. This scene constitutes the climax.
4. His inner tension rises/mounts.
5. The author specifies his ideas as to ...
6. Frankly speaking that is rubbish!
7. The author hints at/alludes to well-known persons.
8. He assumes that ...
9. What puzzles me is that ...
10. The author suggests that ...

Part 9

1. runs as
2. evokes
3. is expected
4. achieve/obtain/attain
5. juxtaposes/contrasts

Revision Test 4

Part 1

1. its
2. believe
3. whose
4. responsibility
5. sense

Part 2

1. That is what I call inhuman.
2. She is very self-assured.
3. He must cope with the situation.
4. It is to be said/It can be said that both are right.
5. We need further information.
6. The text is supposed to be funny?
7. He argues in a very one-sided way.
8. A sensible answer.
9. He will perhaps come.
10. A likeable fellow.

Part 3

1. sheds
2. assume
3. Apparently
4. convinced
5. adds to
6. creates
7. are centred around
8. noticed
9. detailed
10. sticks

Part 4

1. with
2. about
3. on
4. to
5. to

Part 5

1. That is an allegation. Where is your proof?
2. He comes to the conclusion that …
3. Her style is sober and matter-of-fact.
4. His examples are vivid.
5. The author makes a distinction between …
6. He refrains from giving a personal comment.
7. That is precisely the reason why …
8. ‘A’ is at war with himself.

9. The conflict remains unsettled/unsolved.
10. She refutes the argument that ...

Part 6

a)
1. flatly refused/plainly refused
2. entirely/completely wrong
3. vividly object
4. profoundly/deeply concerned
5. extremely difficult

b)
1. reveals
2. draws
3. wins
4. holds
5. takes

Part 7

1. criteria
2. comprises
3. has had
4. can do
5. reminds me of
6. make the reader change
7. I would say that
8. In contrast to me
9. noticed
10. colloquial

Part 8

1. true
2. really
3. real
4. deeply
5. ironically

Die „zehn Todsünden" des Grundkursschülers

Exercise 1

a)
1. He does not want to give up.
2. He need not wait.
3. He must not/is not allowed to fail.
4. She does not believe me.
5. She plans to go to England.
6. She asks him if he has time/has got time.

b)
1. I have <u>been</u> ill.
2. Tomorrow at 8 o'clock we probably will <u>be</u> playing tennis.
3. Otherwise that would have <u>been</u> clear.
4. He said he would have known it if he had <u>been</u> calmer.
5. He must not <u>be</u> forgotten; he has <u>been</u> told that we'll <u>be</u> there.
6. They say I have <u>been</u> made chairman; that must <u>be</u> checked. Otherwise I would <u>be</u> very disappointed.

c)
1. He had been
2. He does not want to be treated
3. He is hated by
4. and reach

5. to make it clear to him
6. answers
7. She told me
8. to spending
9. thought (that) we were safe
10. explains to us
11. wanted the passengers to fasten
12. is interested in
13. make life worth living

Exercise 2

1. Competitive sport would not be so dangerous if sport physiologists acted with more responsibility.
2. If children at the age of three practise seriously, they will often quit when they are thirteen or fourteen years old. They are fed up.
3. Many a youngster would not have lost his/her interest in sport if he/she had not had to practise so hard.
4. If you do not begin early, you will never qualify for national or international championships.
5. Numerous sport stars would not have become so well-known if they had not won in a lot of games.
6. Parents would be better advised if they did not consider their kids as pocket adults.

Exercise 3

1. It is crystal-clear/absolutely clear/totally clear that ...
2. The meaning of the text remains rather dark/obscure to me.
3. You must realize that .../You must become aware that ...
4. He has no choice; he has to cope with/manage/come to grips with the situation.
5. I have only a vague/muddled idea of what the problem is like.
6. I am not quite clear as to what you are aiming at.
7. The author explains it by means of/makes s.th. clear by means of ...
8. Have we removed all unclear points?
9. To me that is a clear-cut proof.

Exercise 4

a)
1. of
2. by ... on
3. against to/of ... of
4. into ... to
5. into ... at
6. of
7. To
8. to
9. on ... ---

b)
1. of
2. in
3. ---
4. to
5. from
6. on
7. according to
8. by
9. between ... and ...
10. From

Exercise 5

1. truly
2. true
3. real
4. really true
5. real
6. really
7. real
8. truly
9. really
10. really
11. true
12. truly

Exercise 6

1. This text is written in the third person.
2. Here substitutionary narration is in action.
3. He also assumes the attitude of an observer.
4. He has to travel the same route day in day out.
5. For him life is depressing and dispiriting.

Exercise 7

1. whose
2. in which
3. whose
4. –––/that
5. who
6. for whom
7. who
8. of which

Exercise 8

1. reading
2. will be
3. fulfilling
4. Joan Collins a star
5. stay
6. meeting

Exercise 9

1. gives/provides
2. wants us to
3. is meant to
4. suggests
5. With
6. either
7. which
8. tells/says to
9. makes
10. a ... of his own
11. thinks/believes
12. make him understand that

Exercise 10

The author
- puts forward/presents/defends
- assumes/supposes/takes for granted
- objects by
- refutes/rejects/disproves the argument that
- provides evidence for/in support of
- gives/provides examples for
- quotes an accepted authority
- refers to/relies on generally accepted/commonly accepted facts
- infers that/deduces that
- draws/comes to/arrives at the conclusion that